MADAME ZADKIEL'S
FORTUNE TELLER & MIRROR OF FATE

Madame Zadkiel's

Fortune Teller

–and–

Mirror of Fate

New Orleans
ARABI MANOR
A Rebel Satori Imprint

THIS EDITION PUBLISHED
IN THE UNITED STATES & UNITED KINGDOM
BY ARABI MANOR
AN IMPRINT OF REBEL SATORI PRESS

ORIGINALLY PUBLISHED IN 1884 BY
EXCELSIOR PUBLISHING HOUSE

ISBN: 978-1-60864-184-0

ORACULUM.

QUESTIONS.	* * *	** * *	* ** *	** * **	** * *	*** ** *	** ** *	** ** **	** ** **	** *** *	* ** **	* ** ***	* *** **	** *** *	* ** **	** ** **
Shall I obtain my wish?	A	B	C	D	E	F	G	H	I	K	L	M	N	O	P	Q
Shall I have success in my business?	B	C	D	E	F	G	H	I	K	L	M	N	O	P	Q	A
Shall I gain or lose in my cause?	C	D	E	F	G	H	I	K	L	M	N	O	P	Q	A	B
Shall I have to live in foreign parts?	D	E	F	G	H	I	K	L	M	N	O	P	Q	A	B	C
Will the stranger return from abroad?	E	F	G	H	I	K	L	M	N	O	P	Q	A	B	C	D
Shall I recover my property stolen?	F	G	H	I	K	L	M	N	O	P	Q	A	B	C	D	E
Will my friend be true in his dealings?	G	H	I	K	L	M	N	O	P	Q	A	B	C	D	E	F
Shall I have to travel?	H	I	K	L	M	N	O	P	Q	A	B	C	D	E	F	G
Does the person love and regard me?	I	K	L	M	N	O	P	Q	A	B	C	D	E	F	G	H
Will the marriage be prosperous?	K	L	M	N	O	P	Q	A	B	C	D	E	F	G	H	I
What sort of a partner shall I have?	L	M	N	O	P	Q	A	B	C	D	E	F	G	H	I	K
Will she have a son or a daughter?	M	N	O	P	Q	A	B	C	D	E	F	G	H	I	K	L
Will the patient recover?	N	O	P	Q	A	B	C	D	E	F	G	H	I	K	L	M
Will the prisoner be released?	O	P	Q	A	B	C	D	E	F	G	H	I	K	L	M	N
Shall I be lucky or unlucky this day?	P	Q	A	B	C	D	E	F	G	H	I	K	L	M	N	O
What does my dream signify?	Q	A	B	C	D	E	F	G	H	I	K	L	M	N	O	P

NAPOLEON'S ORACULUM;

OR,

BOOK OF FATE.

The Oraculum is gifted with every requisite variety of response to the following questions:

1. Shall I obtain my wish?
2. Shall I have succcess in my undertakings?
3. Shall I gain or lose in my cause?
4. Shall I have to live in foreign parts?
5. Will the stranger return?
6. Shall I recover my property?
7. Will my friend be true?
8. Shall I have to travel?
9. Does the person love and regard me?
10. Will the marriage be prosperous?
11. What sort of a wife, or husband, shall I **have?**
12. Will she have a son or daughter?
13. Will the patient recover?
14. Will the prisoner be released?
15. Shall I be lucky or unlucky?
16. What does my dream signify?

HOW TO WORK THE ORACULUM.

Make marks in four lines, one under another, in the following manner, making more or less in each line, according to your fancy:

  * * * * * *
  * * * * * * *
  * * * * * * * *
  * * * * * * * * *

Then reckon the number of marks in each line, and, if it be *odd*, mark down one dot; if *even*, two dots. If there be more than nine marks, reckon the surplus ones over that number only, viz:

The number of marks in the first line of the foregoing are *odd;* therefore, make one mark, thus...................... *
In the second, *even*, so make two, thus................... * *
In the third, *odd* again, make one mark only........... *
In the fourth, *even* again, two marks.................... * *

TO OBTAIN THE ANSWER.

You must refer to the Oraculum, at the top of which you will find a row of dots similar to those you have produced, and a column of figures corresponding with those prefixed to the questions; guide your eye down the column at the top of which you find the dots resembling your own, till you come to the letter on a line with the number of the question you are trying, then refer to the page having that letter at the top, and, on a line with the dots which are similar to your own, you will find your *answer*.

The following are unlucky days, on which none of the questions should be worked, or any enterprise undertaken: Jan. 1, 2, 4, 6, 10, 20, 22; Feb. 6, 17, 28; Mar. 24, 26; April 10, 27, 28; May 7, 8; June 27; July 17, 21; Aug. 20, 22; Sept. 5, 30; Oct. 6; Nov. 3, 29; Dec. 6, 10, 15.

 ₂ It is not right to try a question twice in one day.

A.

✳✳✳✳	What you wish for you will shortly obtain.
✳✳✳✳✳	Signifies trouble and sorrow.
✳✳✳✳	Be very cautious what you do this day, lest trouble befall you.
✳✳✳✳✳	The prisoner dies and is regretted by his friends.
✳✳✳✳✳	Life will be spared this time to prepare for death.
✳✳✳✳✳	A very handsome daughter but a painful one.
✳✳✳✳✳	You will have a virtuous woman or man for your wife or husband.
✳✳✳✳✳	If you marry this person you will have enemies where you little expect.
✳✳✳✳✳	You had better decline this love, for it is neither constant nor true.
✳✳✳✳	Decline your travels for they will not be to your advantage.
✳✳✳✳	There is a true and sincere friendship between you both.
✳✳✳✳	You will not recover the stolen property.
✳✳✳✳	The stranger will, with joy, soon return.
✳✳✳✳	You will not remove from where you are at present.
✳✳✳	Providence will support you in a good cause.
✳✳✳✳✳✳	You are not lucky.

B.

✳	The luck that is ordained for you will be coveted by others.
✳✳	What ever your desires are for the present decline them.
✳✳	Signifies a favor or kindness from some person.
✳✳	There are enemies who would defraud and render you unhappy.
✳✳	With great difficulty he will obtain pardon or release again.
✳✳	The paitent should be prepared to leave this world.
✳✳	She will have a son who will be learned and wise.
✳✳	A rich partner is ordained for you.
✳✳	By this marriage you will have great luck and prosperity.
✳	This love comes from an upright and sincere heart.
✳✳	A higher power will surely travel with you and bless you.
✳	Beware of friends who are false and deceitful.
✳	You will recover your property—unexpectedly.
✳	Love prevents his return home at present.
✳	Your stay is not here, be therefore prepared for a change.
✳✳	You will have no gain, therefore be wise and careful.

C.

✻	With the blessing of God you will have great gain.
✻	Very unlucky indeed—pray for assistance.
✻	If your desires are not extravagant they will be granted.
✻	Signifies peace and plenty between friends.
✻	Be well prepared this day or you may meet with trouble.
✻	The prisoner will find it difficult to obtain his pardon or release.
✻	The patient will yet enjoy health and prosperity.
✻	She will have a daughter and will require attention.
✻	The person has not a great fortune but is in middling circumstances.
✻	Decline this marriage or else you may be sorry.
✻	Decline a courtship which may be your destruction.
✻	Your travels are in vain; you had better stay at home.
✻	You may depend on a true and sincere friendship.
✻	You must not expect to regain that which you have lost.
✻	Sickness prevents the traveler from seeing you.
✻	It will be your fate to stay where you now are.

D.

✳✳✳✳	You will obtain a great fortune in another country.
✳✳✳✳✳	By venturing freely you will certainly gain doubly.
✳✳✳✳	A higher power will change your misfortune into success and happiness.
✳✳✳✳✳	Alter your intentions or else you may meet poverty and distress.
✳✳✳✳✳	Signifies you have many impediments in accomplishing your pursuits.
✳✳✳✳✳	Whatever may possess your inclinations this day abandon them.
✳✳✳✳	The prisoner will get free again this time.
✳✳✳✳✳	The patient's illness will be lingering and doubtful.
✳✳✳✳	She will have a dutiful and handsome son.
✳✳✳✳	The person will be low in circumstances but honest-hearted.
✳✳✳✳	A marriage which will add to your welfare and prosperity.
✳✳✳✳	You love a person who does not speak well of you.
✳✳✳✳	Your travels will be prosperous if guided by prudence.
✳✳✳✳	He means not what he says for his heart is false.
✳✳✳✳	With some trouble and expense you may regain your property.
✳✳✳✳✳✳	You must not expect to see the stranger again.

E.

✳✳✳✳	The stranger will not return so soon as you expect.
✳✳✳✳	Remain among your friends and you will do well.
✳✳✳✳	You will hereafter gain what you seek.
✳✳✳✳	You have no luck—pray and strive honestly.
✳✳✳✳	You will obtain your wishes by means of a friend.
✳✳✳✳	Signifies you have enemies who will endeavor to ruin you.
✳✳✳✳	Beware—an enemy is endeavoring to bring you to strife and misfortune.
✳✳✳✳	The prisoner's sorrow and anxiety are great and his release uncertain.
✳✳✳✳	The patient will soon recover—there is no danger.
✳✳✳✳	She will have a daughter who will be honored and respected.
✳✳✳✳	Your partner will be fond of liquor and will debase himself thereby.
✳✳✳✳	This marriage will bring you poverty be therefore discreet.
✳✳✳✳	Their love is false to you and true to others.
✳✳✳✳	Decline your travels for the present for they will be dangerous.
✳✳✳✳	This person is serious and true and deserves to be respected.
✳✳✳✳	You will not recover the property you have lost.

F.

*****	By persevering you will recover your property again.
*****	It is out of the stranger's power to return.
*****	You will gain and be successful in foreign parts.
*****	A great fortune is ordained for you, wait patiently.
*****	There is great hindrance to your success at present.
*****	Your wishes are in vain at present.
*****	Signifies there is sorrow and danger before you.
*****	This day is unlucky, therefore alter your intention.
*****	The prisoner will be restored to liberty and freedom.
*****	The patient's recovery is doubtful.
*****	She will have a very fine boy.
*****	A worthy person and a fine fortune.
*****	Your intentions would destroy your rest and peace.
*****	The love is true and constant, forsake it not.
*****	Proceed on your journey and you will not have cause to repent it.
*****	If you trust this friend you may have cause for sorrow.

I.

✳✳✳✳	The love is great, but will cause great jealousy.
✳✳✳✳	It will be in vain for you to travel.
✳✳✳✳	Your friend will be as sincere as you could wish him to be.
✳✳✳✳	You will recover the stolen property through a cunning person.
✳✳✳✳	The traveler will soon return with joy.
✳✳✳✳	You will not be prosperous or fortunate in foreign parts.
✳✳✳✳	Place your trust in God, who is the disposer of happiness.
✳✳✳✳	Your fortune will shortly be changed into misfortune.
✳✳✳✳	You will succeed as you desire.
✳✳✳✳	Signifies that the misfortune which threatens will be prevented.
✳✳✳✳	Beware of your enemies, who seek to do you harm.
✳✳✳✳	After a short time, your anxiety for the prisoner will cease.
✳✳✳✳	God will give the patient health and strength again.
✳✳✳✳	She will have a very fine daughter.
✳✳✳✳	You will marry a person with whom you will have little comfort.
✳✳✳✳	The marriage will not answer your expectations.

K.

✳✳✳✳	After much misfortune, you will be comfortable and happy.
✳✳✳✳	A sincere love from an upright heart.
✳✳✳✳	You will be prosperous in your journey.
✳✳✳✳	Do not rely on the friendship of this person.
✳✳✳✳	The property is lost for ever; but the thief will be punished.
✳✳✳✳	The traveler will be absent some considerable time.
✳✳✳✳	You will meet luck and happiness in a foreign country.
✳✳✳✳	You will not have any success for the present.
✳✳✳✳	You will succeed in your undertaking.
✳✳✳✳	Change your intentions, and you will do well.
✳✳✳✳	Signifies that there are rogues at hand.
✳✳✳✳	Be reconciled, your circumstances will shortly mend.
✳✳✳✳	The prisoner will be released.
✳✳✳✳	The patient will depart this life.
✳✳✳✳	She will have a son.
✳✳✳✳	It will be difficult for you to get a partner.

L.

✱✱✱✱	You will get a very handsome person for your partner.
✱✱✱✱✱	Various misfortunes will attend this marriage.
✱✱✱✱	This love is whimsical and changeable.
✱✱✱✱✱✱	You will be unlucky in your travels.
✱✱✱✱✱✱✱	This person's love is true. You may rely on it.
✱✱✱✱✱✱	You will lose, but the thief will suffer most.
✱✱✱✱✱	The stranger will soon return with plenty.
✱✱✱✱✱✱✱	If you remain at home, you will have success.
✱✱✱✱	Your gain will be trivial.
✱✱✱✱	You will meet sorrow and trouble.
✱✱✱✱✱✱	You will succeed according to your wishes.
✱✱✱✱✱	Signifies that you will get money.
✱✱✱✱	In spite of enemies, you will do well.
✱✱✱	The prisoner will pass many days in confinement.
✱✱✱✱	The patient will recover.
✱✱✱✱✱✱	She will have a daughter.

※※※	She will have a son, who will gain wealth and honor.
※※※※※	You will get a partner with great undertakings and much money.
※※※※※	The marriage will be prosperous.
※※※※※	She, or he, wishes to be yours this moment.
※※※※※	Your journey will prove to your advantage.
※※※※※	Place no great trust in that person.
※※※※※	You will find your property at a certain time.
※※※※※	The traveler's return is rendered doubtful by his conduct.
※※※※※	You will succeed as you desire in foreign parts.
※※※※	Expect no gain; it will be in vain.
※※※※※	You will have more luck than you expect.
※※※※※	Whatever your desires are, you will speedily obtain them.
※※※※	Signifies you will be asked to a wedding.
※※※	You will have no occasion to complain of ill-luck.
※※※	Some one will pity and release the prisoner.
※※※※※	The patient's recovery is unlikely.

N

✳✳✳✳	The patient will recover, but his days are short.
✳✳ ✳ ✳✳ ✳	She will have a daughter.
✳ ✳✳ ✳✳ ✳	You will marry into a very respectable family.
✳✳ ✳ ✳ ✳✳	By this marriage you will gain nothing.
✳✳ ✳✳ ✳✳ ✳	Await the time and you will find the love great.
✳✳ ✳✳ ✳✳	Venture not from home.
✳✳ ✳ ✳ ✳	This person is a sincere friend.
✳✳ ✳✳ ✳ ✳	You will never recover the theft.
✳ ✳ ✳✳ ✳✳	The stranger will return, but not quickly.
✳ ✳ ✳ ✳✳	When abroad, keep from evil women or they will do you harm.
✳✳ ✳ ✳✳ ✳✳	You will soon gain what you little expect.
✳ ✳✳ ✳✳ ✳✳	You will have great success.
✳ ✳✳ ✳	Rejoice ever at that which is ordained for you.
✳ ✳✳ ✳✳	Signifies that sorrow will depart, and joy will return.
✳ ✳ ✳✳	Your luck is in blossom; it will soon be at hand.
✳✳ ✳✳ ✳✳ ✳✳	Death may end the imprisonment.

O.

✱✱✱✱	The prisoner will be released with joy.
✱✱ ✱✱ ✱	The patient's recovery is doubtful.
✱ ✱✱ ✱✱	She will have a son, who will live to a great age.
✱✱ ✱ ✱✱	You will get a virtuous partner.
✱✱ ✱✱ ✱✱ ✱	Delay not this marriage—you will meet much happiness.
✱✱ ✱✱ ✱ ✱✱	None loves you better in this world.
✱✱ ✱ ✱ ✱	You may proceed with confidence.
✱✱ ✱✱ ✱ ✱	Not a friend, but a secret enemy.
✱ ✱✱ ✱✱	You will soon recover what is stolen.
✱ ✱ ✱ ✱✱	The stranger will not return again.
✱✱ ✱✱ ✱✱	A foreign woman will greatly enhance your fortune.
✱ ✱✱ ✱✱ ✱✱	You will be cheated out of your gain.
✱ ✱✱ ✱✱ ✱	Your misfortunes will vanish and you will be happy.
✱ ✱ ✱ ✱	Your hope is in vain—fortune shuns you at present.
✱ ✱ ✱ ✱✱	That you will soon hear agreeable news.
✱✱ ✱✱ ✱✱ ✱✱	There are misfortunes lurking about you.

P.

****	This day brings you an increase of happiness.
****	The prisoner will quit the power of his enemies.
****	The patient will recover and live long.
****	She will have two daughters.
****	A rich young person will be your partner.
****	Hasten your marriage—it will bring you much happiness.
****	The person loves you sincerely.
****	You will not prosper from home.
****	This friend is more valuable than gold.
****	You will never receive your goods.
****	He is dangerously ill, and cannot yet return.
****	Depend upon your own industry, and remain at home.
****	Be joyful, for future prosperity is ordained for you.
****	Depend not too much on your good luck.
****	What you wish will be granted to you.
****	That you should be very careful this day, least any accident befall you.

Q.

✻	Signifies much joy and happiness between friends.
✻	This day is not very lucky, but rather the reverse.
✻	He will yet come to honor, although he now suffers.
✻	Recovery is doubtful; therefore be prepared for the worst.
✻	She will have a son who will prove forward.
✻	A rich partner but a bad temper.
✻	By wedding this person you insure your happiness.
✻	The person has great love for you, but wishes to conceal it.
✻	You may proceed on your journey without fear.
✻	Trust him not; he is inconstant and deceitful.
✻	In a very singular manner you will recover your property.
✻	The stranger will return very soon.
✻	You will dwell abroad in comfort and happiness.
✻	If you will deal fairly you will surely prosper.
✻	You will yet live in splendor and plenty.
✻	Make yourself contented with your present fortune.

THE COUNTESS OF BLESSINGTON'S

TRUE INTERPRETER OF

DREAMS, VISIONS, OMENS OF THE WEDDING DAY, &c., &c.

INTERPRETATION OF DREAMS,

And their real signification in connection with all the events that may happen to the person dreaming, and the affairs of relatives, friends, or enemies, from birth to death!

A.

An angel on the wing,
Death to the sick doth bring;
To those in health much joy—man, woman, girl, or boy.

Ants show you'll have good trade without adversity;
Visits from strangers, much profit and prosperity.

Adultery will lead you to danger and strife,
But affliction will bring you to a joyful life.

An anchor fixed, in your dream, will hinder your scheme,
But when uplifted, your elevation doth seem.

Alliances with people, denotes quarrelling, quite,
To learn the alphabet, lucky—not if you write;
But to print it, will bring you in business, success,
Alms to the poor gives joy, to the rich much distress.

To see apples, shows a wedding; to eat sour ones, bad,
But sweet ones will make you with prosperity glad.

Adders, if you dream of, denote many good friends,
To bid adieu is honor, and prosperous ends.

Broken arms shows danger, great or long arms, friendship;
But small ones, enemies, who will your prosperity strip.

To see an ass is bad luck, to ride one is scorn,
To load an ass shows much toil; to beat one, you'll mourn.

Arms, denote losses, armor, security forebodes,
Arrows show bad luck, that you'll die poor on the roads.

A cloudy morning twilight, shows ill luck, and grief,
A bright sunny one will bring good news and relief

B.

Bacon, if you dream of, no good luck you will get,
To catch a badger, you'll prosperity see yet;
And if you wear on you a nice warm badger's skin,
You shall for your heritage, a fine house live in.

To see baking is famine, if you bake, 'tis good,
Plenty of wealth you'll have, house, garden, fields, and wood

To dream you hear dogs barking, is a grievous sign,
A barber denotes, under losses you shall whine.

Walking barefooted, denotes poverty and loss,
Bathing in rivers, good fortune, if you don't cross;
Clear water is best, a pond, unlucky, indeed,
Muddy water shows crosses, suffering and need.

A barn indicates a store of money and food,
And bats denote great storms, and strife, and news not good

To dream of battle's rage, is joy and pleasure,
Birds denote luck in play, and a heap of treasure.

To eat beans is a sign of quarrels and disdain,
Bears doth show much calumny, backbiting and pain.

To dream of men with long beards, great honor doth show,
But with short beards, contempt and poverty you'll know.

Black beards, gain in play; gray or red, illness and pain,
Mustaichos show toil and trouble you shall only gain.

THE PERFECT FORTUNE TELLER.

To dream of a bearded woman, signifies death,
Or that you are beaten, some accident, and bad health.

Beavers are sure signs of bad enemies and lies,
Beds that are handsome, show riches shall be your prize.

But a mean bed shows that poor you will be through life,
Lying in bed forebodes illness to yourself and wife

To dream of a beggar, a present is the sign,
To relieve beggars shows prosperity is thine.

To dream of begging, an inheritance doth show,
To see one beheaded, you will die of a blow.

To dream you hear bells, is a sign of enmity
And if you ring them they will cause you misery.

Large bellows blows you good news, but the small ones bad,
To blow them yourself, you shall quarrel and be sad.

To see roaring billows, betokens dangers great,
Birds shot flying are false news, to catch them shows hate.

Dreaming of bird's nests, or eggs, show good luck is thine,
But if then you eat them, in sorrow you will pine.

Bishops, show law suits, if they talk your cause succeeds,
To dream of black, the heart, with sorrow always bleeds.

Biting, denotes controversy and loud wrangling,
Bleaching linen, shows death, and dirty clothes, jangling;
To dream of being bled is of sickness a sure sign,
And though you bind the vein, loss, harm, and griefs are thine

If you dream that you are blind, misfortunes are near,
Or of spitting blood, long illness you may fear.

To hear the wind blow, hate and quarreling denotes,
But music from wind instruments, friendship promotes.

To read good books, signifies presents you'll receive,
But bad ones will cause all your family to grieve.

Dreaming of a bookbinder, foretells prosperous times,
To dream of births, or being born, are fortunate signs.

Dreaming of being bound, or tied, is a sign of need,
Box trees show great sorrow, and ill-paid work indeed.

THE PERFECT FORTUNE TELLER.

Breeches to wear is honor, to man, maid or dame,
To tear them brings misfortune—to every one shame.

Drinking brandy, portends joyful news is near,
Eating or buying bread, starvation never fear.

Dreaming of a bridge, is elevation in life,
If broken down, it shows difficulties and strife.

Glittering things are sure signs of ruin and perdition,
Brimstone shows bad luck and a wretched condition.

Seeing a large deep brook is vexation and sorrow,
Clear water running through the house, good news to-morrow

Seeing and speaking to a brother shows ill luck long,
Dreaming of buckles doth portend anger and wrong.

To dream of buildings shows old age, with a good wife,
Buried alive portends that you will lose your life.

Seeing things burning bright denotes prosperity,
When it only glimmers, rage and perversity.

Dry bush or underwood shows distress and grief,
Green bushes, to trouble, promises relief.

C.

Dreaming of a calf denotes prosperous you'll be,
And a camel shows quarrelling will soon plague thee.

Cans or tankards show pleasant news—to drink is well,
Wax candles are lucky, tallow ones bad luck tell.

Speaking or acting with candor, good fortune show,
Card playing is a sign of displeasure and woe.

A carriage is honor, but to break down is strife,
Carrion is a sign of good times and a long life.

Cats are enemies, bitten by them bad luck shows,
If they should scratch you, they will bring upon you woes.

To caress them they are as false as they can be,
To kill one is a triumph over an enemy.

THE PERFECT FORTUNE TELLER.

Dreaming of cattle shows you'll be richer than I,
Caterpillars doth losses in trade signify.

To see a cavern portends that your joy is short,
Living in one room shows poverty, as it ought.

Dreaming of sitting on a chair denotes great respect,
Chains showeth imprisonment, bad news, death and neglect.

To become a chaplain shows elevation high,
Cheese signifies good luck, to make it is to die.

Cherries denote a quarrelsome husband or wife,
Children are not good, if they die, 'tis good for life.

Dreaming of women confined, does a death portend,
A chimney sweeper shows good luck will you attend.

Drinking of hot chocolate will bring you delight,
To adore Christ will signify joy day and night.

A church denotes disaster, praying therein is well,
And to build a church, some one's death it doth foretell.

Dreaming of the clergy, is a long life to you
Clocks are good, but if they strike, will your luck undo.

Clothes, when they are clean, of prosperity doth tell,
But those unclean, show sickness and some funeral knell.

Torn clothes forebodes quarrelling, fine clothes, station high,
Mean clothes denotes that in poverty you will sigh.

Thick and heavy clouds show some error you'll commit,
Clear clouds, under your own tree happy you will sit.

To see a coach is honor, to ride is treachery,
But a coach overturned, elevated you'll be.

Seeing lighted coals is money and a large estate,
But dreaming of cinders shows death will seal your fate.

To see cocks is good news, if they crow, better still,
And hens laying eggs will with gold your pockets fill

To dream of drinking coffee quarrelling doth show,
Collecting and gathering goods, is humbling to you.

THE PERFECT FORTUNE TELLER.

To dream of a comb is unfortunate indeed,
And to comb your hair, I your future sorrow read.

Men's coats show riches, women's gowns, the marriage bell
To see a comedy acted, back-biting doth tell.

To console persons at funerals shows a sick bed,
To be consoled yourself is, by fire you'll fall dead.

To bind things with a cord is profit and employ,
To dream of seeing ears of corn is a sure sign of joy.

But to pluck corn warns you of secret enemies,
Fields of corn, or cutting it, shows with friends you'll rise.

To dream of a corpse is a fortune to you quite,
Conversing with a Count, humiliation downright.

To dream of counting things is quite unfortunate,
Milking or killing cows foretells your prosperous state.

Lean cows doth poverty, also famine, foreshow,
Fat cows with plenty will your cupboards overflow.

Dreaming of crabs is a prosperous journey for you,
Catching or eating them, your fortune shall undo.

Dreaming of being crown'd is loss and excitement bad,
To pray shows a pious wife, a cross, that you'll be glad.

To dream of any cruelty denotes good news, and strange,
A cuckoo's cry shows evil tongues will you derange.

D.

To dream of dancing denotes weariness and strife,
Darkness, forebodes a long and lingering sickly life.

A dark lantern reflects your secret enemies,
Being dead is good fortune, joy, if another dies.

Dreaming of being deaf it your marriage doth portend,
Being in debt shows an estate and a lucky end.

Deer denote the good news that your fortune is made,
To see the devil proves you'll get riches by trade.

THE PERFECT FORTUNE TELLER.

Digging graves doth portend a wedding propitious,
Dice showeth discord and that your luck is vicious.

Dishes prepared for eating a famine portend,
To dream of a distaff sickness soon you shall end.

To dream of digging a ditch a long journey you'll take,
If dogs bark or bite you in fear of death you'll quake.

Little dogs are good friends, great ones enemies bad,
Mangy dogs show sickness, mad ones will make you sad.

Dream of many servants is a sickly dream,
To see dragons is scorn and ruin to your best scheme.

Drinking plainly foretells squandering money away,
Ducks show inundation, to catch them is bad to-day.

To seem dumb is dignity, and good luck to all,
Dung shows good times and that plenty on you shall fall.

E.

To see an eagle fly denotes gain and success,
But if an eagle, sit or stand 'tis death and distress;
If you shoot them you shall have losses by a thief,
Or, if you catch them, you shall feel illness and grief.

To dream of the ears is joy—long ears, confusion,
Earwigs are signs of lawyers and prosecution.

Earthquakes denote great changes in your future fate,
Eating good meals shows famine, bad ones strife and hate.

To buy eggs is ill-luck, to boil them a mistake,
To dream you make enclosures your fortune you'll make.

An elephant denotes honor and gain to all,
To dream of conquering enemies shows their downfall.

To sell any estate is a misfortune great,
But to buy one foretells a more fortunate fate.

Blue eyes portend joy, evil-looking, success in trade,
Large handsome eyes show your fortune will be soon made.

Thick eyebrows is a sign you will ne'er want a friend,
And black brows show good luck, thin ones, a bad end.

THE PERFECT FORTUNE TELLER.

F.

To see a face in a looking-glass is long life,
But to see it in water is hatred and strife.

Yourself falling is bad—others, elevating,
Fruit dropping from trees show ill-luck and vexation.

Fallen trees and wood is honor, while you draw breath,
But if you dream you fall 'tis sure sign of death

Your father is fortunate, his death is ill-gain,
Lovers fighting is joy, old people, death and pain.

Fighting with swords deliverance and freedom doth show,
To the debtor gives help, and relief from his woe.

To wear a plume of feathers is honor in life,
But to trade in them portends anxiety and strife.

Pain in the finger shows good fortune for you,
But to cut it, unlucky; which you'll find is true.

Seeing fire bright and clear shows happiness is near,
To dream of fire-arms some quarreling you must fear.

To be in a forest of fir-trees shows much pining,
Catching fish tells of crosses, and your trade declining.

Foals, flowers, or flying in the air, are good omens to all
Catching fleas denotes much trouble will you befall.

Flax a good marriage shows, spinning it brings troubles,
Birds, flesh, flies or foxes, denote your hopes are bubbles.

To dream of friends or a forge is a bad sign,
To tell some ones fortune shows ill-luck will be thine.

Frogs, or fruit, indicates riches and a long life,
Furs portend you'll wealthy be, with a handsome wife.

G.

To dream of a garnet or coral, shows great care,
Gaiety, fortells trouble to the dark and fair.

Glass or cut grass, bring crosses to husband and wife,
Goats or gnats, show the plots of false friends throughout life

THE PERFECT FORTUNE TELLER.

To receive guests or see ghosts, portends speedy death,
Or if a guest yourself, famine will stop your breath.

To dream you govern is a fortune you will save,
The death of your wife that you will go to the grave.

To vomit gall denotes you'll receive help in need,
Gardens show riches, from a workhouse you are freed.

Gaming shows bad news, losing in play is great gain,
To dream of gold will bring luck, is a sign always plain.

Geese, killed, roasted or eaten, joy, health and wealth bring
To dream of a gleaner with content you'll sing.

A nice grass plat is, of a fine marriage the sign,
Cattle grazing denotes that good-luck shall be thine.

Grandfathers and mothers, portend wealth and long life,
To see green color brings luck to you and your wife.

H

Hangmen and hanging, misfortunes and sickness show,
If struck by hailstones much grief and illness you'll know.

To dream you cut your own hair unlucky you will be,
White or black shows good-luck, but short, is poverty.

Red hair stamps deceit, brown, the sensual and rude,
Hair on hands unlucky is, long hair, disquietude.

Hall of Justice, or harp-playing, shows envy and need,
To shave or cut off heads, a relation's death read.

Heath or forest, denotes some great enemy,
Hemp shows ill-fate, hell, damage to property.

Hares or hens, without young, brings pain and agony
With young, or to shoot, or eat them, pleasure you'll see.

Cackling hens, hawks, or cattle, long life and success,
Clean hands show good fortune, dirty, much untidiness.

Luck and joy comes with horsemen, horse, or horse-shoes,
To ride, or to see them, are riches and good news.

But, if drawn by them, many cares you'll live to see,
While dead horses indicate much adversity.

Huntsmen, show enemies, howling is a sign of joy,
Husbandry, signifies pleasure without alloy.

Full hives, mean riches, empty ones much poverty,
To see, or pull down old houses, sick you shall be;
But to dream of buying them, is lucky to all,
And bad luck comes to those who sell, or see them fall

I.

Using ink, shows misery, ivory is a bad sign,
A life of grief ivy denotes, always shall be thine.

If you dream of infanticide by your own hand,
You'll travel, and be prosperous in a foreign land.

J.

To see Jews or Jewesses, bad luck doth beseem,
To sell or lose jewels, is an unlucky dream;
For great loses you'll have, but to buy them, is gain,
To dream of joyful news, is death, sickness, and pain.

Being joyous and merry, none but quarrels are thine,
A judge, shows you'll get money—a very good sign.

K.

Keys denote power, to see them, fortunate you'll be,
Killing animals, show some accident to thee.

Kings, or queens, mean honor, their death, many crosses
To dream of kids, show, in your trade you'll have losses.

L.

A woman in labor, shows deliverance at hand,
Lambs, indicate pleasure, riches, houses, and land.

To go up a ladder, high in life you'll ascend,
But to descend the same you'll come to bad end.

To dream of lame people, you'll succeed in life well,
Lamps, or lanterns; or larks, of good friends and luck tell.

Dreaming of laths, is sickness, laughing shows luck bad,
To have dealings with lawyers, portend anguish sad.

THE PERFECT FORTUNE TELLER.

Leaden bullets, or learning, some good news doth show,
Large green leaves, show health, dead ones, sickness and wife.

Leeches, lentils, or locusts, famine, want, and sorrow,
Leprosy, shows illness to-day, and death to-morrow.

To receive, or read letters, good news comes in haste,
Love, shows fortune, and joy, with a pretty wife, chaste.

Seeing a bright light is good, and to strike one is gain,
To dream of lions, or lizards, good friends showeth plain.

To dream of linen, you'll ne'er ride in your carriage,
But lillies are a sign of a prosperous marriage.

Dreaming of liver, denotes you'll soon resign breath,
A looking-glass shows naught good, but generally death.

M.

Mad people, or merchants, foretell profit and joy,
To salute a young maid, trouble shall you annoy.

To put on a mantle, shows a situation,
To put off one, is disappointment and vexation.

To dream of going to market, is a sickly sign,
And to eat roast meat, death and misfortune are thine;
But to buy it, at cards you shall be a winner,
Mice, shows great gain and that you'll ne'er want a dinner

Dreaming of a mad wife treachery does indicate,
Milk shows triumph over enemies, and a prosperous fate.

Flour and other mills are lucky, coffee mills, bad,
A miller signifies good friends who'll make you glad.

An unpleasant visit you'll have, if miners you see,
To dig mines is hard work and little profit to thee.

Being miserable or seeing misery denotes disgrace,
Or mixing up things you may therein quarrels trace.

Monks indicate many crosses and vexation,
Seeing or getting money, joy, marriage and station.

To dream of great heaps shows losses and sorrow.
To find money (not gold) bad luck to-morrow.

THE PERFECT FORTUNE TELLER.

Monkeys portend sickness, also success in love,
If they dance you'll be as happy as a young dove.

A clear moon shows much gain—a fiery one, honor,
A red moon, a good wife to love and dote on her;
If a halo around it, you'll succeed in play,
But if 'tis pale or clouded, unlucky next day.

Women dreaming of mortar, their husbands shall beat,
But the men shall prosper and have plenty to eat.

To see your own mother is a fortunate dream,
And high mountains denotes great honor and esteem.

Mushrooms forebode happiness of short duration,
To hear music is sorrow and tribulation.

To see murder shows long life—a murderer, good news,
Mowing is sickness and death to Christians and Jews.

N.

Pleasant news will come if you hear call'd your own name,
Others naked show wealth—yourself naked is shame

Needles, point at hatred, to thread them inquietude,
Nightingales show deceit, over which you shall brood.

A negro indicates joyful tidings for you,
Women's nipples show love and you'll pass well life through

To dream of playing at nine-pins is a lucky sign,
A nun signifies high station and wealth shall be thine.

O.

If you dream of seeing old men fortunate you'll be,
But old women shall cause much vexation to thee.

Old clothes signify fire—perhaps very next morn,
Old buildings show contempt, trouble, losses and scorn.

An oak forest fortells great success in business,
But oats or onions, much suffering, want and distress.

THE PERFECT FORTUNE TELLER.

To dream you trade with oil is fortunate indeed,
An organ shows prosperity—to play, want and need
If they are mournful tunes, but merry ones are good,
A full orchard tells you'll have houses land and wood.

To heat, or bake in an oven good tidings doth show,
To see owls or hear them screech portends to you woe.

To feed, buy, or slay oxen, shows riches shall you bless,
If they toss any one, in love you'll meet success.

P.

Packages show trouble with your children you'll see,
Palm-trees signify wealth and honor comes to thee.

Parade or pomp denotes some unlucky accident,
To dream of parents, money will be to you sent.

To pay bills foretells you'll starve in rags without shoes,
But to see Paradise is a sign of joyful news.

Ripe peaches or pears betoken fortune and friends,
Pearls bring all people tears and foretell their bad ends.

To dream of peasants signifies sociality,
Pictures show deceit, to sell them, prosperity.

Pigeons denote a happy life with friends sincere,
A pitcher broken is death—to drink from, sickness and fear

To dream you pity some one is adversity,
A plough or planks denote a wedding you shall see.

Poison signifies death, misfortunes and a snare,
Pomegranates portend grief, vexation and care.

To se crowds of poor people tells of quarrelling,
Porcelain shows o'er winnings at play you'll loudly sing.

To draw some one's portrait a lucky journey you'll take,
Drawing your own shows that a fortune you will make.

To dream of a potter shows misfortune and death,
Pots signifiy good friends, poverty, famine and death

THE PERFECT FORTUNE TELLER.

To dream that you preach, it much illness doth foretell,
But to hear others preach, in life you shall do well.

To imagine yourself pregnant forebodes much grief,
To take presents is distress—to give one, relief.

To talk to a prince is lucky, dangerous also,
A prison shows deceit and much trouble you shall know.

Printing tells of quarrels about an inheritance,
And profit in trade denotes a good sustenance.

Dreaming of prostitutes foretells shame and disgrace,
Gathering of plums or prunes denotes pride, power and place

To dream you are in prison, from trouble you'll be freed,
To trade with iron or use iron tools, shows pain, death, and need

Q.

Fourfooted quadrupeds doth denote friends faithful,
Quails are like troublesome guests whose company is hateful.

To dream of a queen shows friends, honor or estate,
Quarrelling, illness and other evils indicate.

R.

To dream of torture by the rack is a good sign,
Rainbows make the poor rejoice and the rich to whine.

Rats, ravens, or reeds show ill-will, death and disgrace,
Red colors show quarreling, riches, troubles apace.

Rising of the dead shows honors you may look for,
Riding in a coach—you'll rise and be poor no more.

To dream of large rings put in prison you shall be,
Small finger-rings denotes grandeur you will see.

To lose a ring is sickness, to receive one strife,
Gold rings bring great honor, silver rings a quiet life.

To rise from bed forebodes sickness, from the ground, care,
And good news if you dream that you rise from a chair.

THE PERFECT FORTUNE TELLER.

Narrow and crooked roads are unlucky, very,
Broad and even roads shows you'll travel through life merry.

Running signifies pursuit and much vexation,
A rupture shows loss in trade and tribulation.

Good will with enemies rushing of water shows,
And a lucky sign it is to dream of repose.

S.

To dream of a sabre is great elevation,
Sacks show good tidings to folks in any station.

To dream of salad or salt is of sickness the sign,
And salve or ointment denotes much ill-will shall be thine.

To dream of scales or scissors is a sign of good trade,
Scissor-grinders show friends who will render you aid.

Watch-seals denote employ, money and a carriage,
A scratch or a cut is a sign of marriage.

Schools or shambles portend fighting and vexation,
A shepherd denotes a peaceable station.

Sheep are signs of plenty, to guard them brings luck rare,
Ships foretell good fortune to the dark and the fair.

To dream you suffer shipwreck shows care and crosses,
To put a shirt on, gain, to pull one off, losses.

Seeing a shoemaker or shoes is death and mourning,
Shooting or shot is also anger and storming.

Shops signify in business you'll lose every hour,
Dangers in storms expect when you dream of a shower.

Silk brings luck to man, woman, girl, or boy,
Silver forebodes good trade and matrimonial joy.

To dream of clear skies your trade is but a bubble
Skeletons or skins of animals betoken much trouble.

To see a sleeping-room is a fortunate sign,
But to dream of sliding, nought but troubles are thine.

THE PERFECT FORTUNE TELLER.

To think you've the small-pox, money you will receive,
Smoke from fire denotes dissensions and that you'll grieve

Snails show envy, useless toil, and transportation,
Snakes, that you have enemies and tribulation.

Anger and quarrels are signified by a spear,
Spectacles, to wear them, indicates honor near.

To dream you see spinning shows an unsettled state,
Springs of water denote long life and riches great.

Large squares show great estates, small squares, adversity,
Squirrels, a prosperous marriage blest with a family.

To see stags is fortunate, to shoot them, not so,
Bright stars show great delight, dull stars, sorrow and woe

Stepfather or mother showeth persecution,
To seem walking on stilts, trouble and delusion.

Stones show that you will discover your enemies,
Storks betoken many good friends and true allies.

To strike a person is good luck, yourself struck is bad,
A bright sun gladdens the poor but makes the rich sad.

To dream of suckling shows to poor prosperity,
To the single, marriage, and to the rich, adversity.

To dream of swans or swine is joy to dark or fair,
Or to see swallows fly is a sure sign of care.

Dreaming of a stable shows trouble and anguish,
Swimming signifies you'll soon obtain your wish.

T.

To dream of a table denotes luck and gladness,
Tailors always show great cares, trouble and madness.

Tears denote you'll obtain a good situation,
Teeth falling out is good, to break them, vexation;
To put them in is bad luck, you'll resign your breath,
Hollow teeth are good friends, to swallow them is death.

THE PERFECT FORTUNE TELLER

A tempest and a ship distress't are dangerous signs,
Thieves show bad trade and losses, and unhappy times.

Thirst denotes useless hopes, to quench your thirst is joy
If you cannot quench it, illness will you annoy.

Thorns and thistles doth calamnities betoken,
To suppose your throat is sore shows joy unbroken.

If you dream of tickling, and you'r sick, don't wonder,
Good news from a friend is shown by hearing thunder.

To eat your tongue is death, toads are unfortunate,
Torches show funerals, to wipe on towels a bad fate.

To see towns is favorable, to travel through them care,
Trading, in traveling, bad luck to the dark or fair.

To dream of digging up treasures is unfortunate,
To find, shows gladness, to collect, a wretched state.

Trees loaded with fruit success in business doth show,
Green trees honor and riches, decayed ones much woe,
To cut down another's trees, enemies you'll defeat,
Full blossm'd trees shows your happiness is complete.

To stand, or be brought before courts is vexation,
A truck is a sign of want and tribulation.

Turnips show to both sexes, ill toil and bad ends,
To dream of tinder betokens many good friends.

U.

To dream of a unicorn is unfortunate,
Unchastity promises a fortunate fate.

Unquietness shows good to man, woman, girl or boy,
For, all who dream of it, shall have plenty and joy.

V.

To dream of vaults wherein are dead, sorrow portends,
Venison shows to rich ill luck, to poor a sad end.

THE PERFECT FORTUNE TELLER.

Villages, ill-paid toil and bad luck signify,
Travelling through them is suffering, perhaps to die;
If one burn, 'tis welfare; vines, a happy marriage,
And if you pluck the grapes you'll ride in your carriage.

To dream you hear a violin play shows happiness,
To play on it, anger, disasters and distress.

W.

To believe you're a wagoner it doth good beseem,
To see one, or wander, an unlucky dream.

Wasps denote enemies; war is a lucky sign,
To dream of washing denotes plenty shall be thine.

Dreaming of watchmen or policemen treachery denote,
Thick dirty water shows with trouble you'll be smote

Clear cold water foretells that you'll be fortunate,
Deep is dangerous, hot, show snares, frozen, a good fate.

All weapons mean evil tongues and snares laid for you,
A weasel shows a quarrelsome wife you'll be wedded to.

To dream of being wedded unfortunate you'll be,
To be at another's wedding brings luck to thee.

To dig a well indicates trouble and sorrow,
A wen on the neck tells of a death to-morrow.

To dream of weavers at work bespeaks a good fate,
To buy corn, inquietude, to sell, a happy state.

To see one wheel, shows in marriage, vexation,
Many wheels portend fortune, joy and high station.

If you dream of a widow it foretells good news,
Or widower—you'll wed the best wife you can choose.

A man to dream he takes a wife shows prosperity,
To see her die, that he'll be free from adversity.

To dream you see wild beasts much happiness indicates,
A window open doth to successful work relate.

Luck is shown in drinking wine, news in a wine-glass,
A wine-cellar shows your sick bed where months you'll pass.

THE PERFECT FORTUNE TELLER.

To dream that you hear the wind roar is happiness,
Or, to wish for anything, false news and distress.

To dream of wood or woolens denotes easy life,
A wolf or worms show hidden enemies and strife.

Dress'd as a woman shows want, hidden enemies and lies,
But to kiss one, much luck and gain it signifies;
To only see a woman is talk, false and sly,
And separation from friends when you see one die.

Being in a wood is a sign you will mourning wear,
Wrestling or wrangling shows fighting, sickness and care.

To dream of a wreath is scorn, without flowers is woe,
But if you are writing no want you shall e'er know.

Y.

To dream you'r young shows you'll soon resign your breath,
Yew trees is a certain sign of sickness and death.

To carry yarn to the weaver denotes travelling,
To dream of youths or yeomen much money you'll win.

ALECTROMANCY.

Trace a circle and inscribe upon its edge the letters of the alphabet. Place a grain of wheat upon each letter. Place a cock in the center of the circle and note down the letters corresponding to the grains as he swallows them. Unite them together and you have a satisfactory answer to the question proposed. Care must be taken to replace the grains as the cock devours them, for the same letter may be repeated many times in the same phrase.

The Emperor Valentine made use of this definition to ascertain who would be his successor. The grains swallowed by the cock, corresponded to the letters T, H, E, O, D. He consequently concluded the sovereignty would be claimed by Theodorus, his secretary, whom he caused to be put to death. But the prediction was nevertheless verified, because Theodosius, the Great, succeeded Valentius.

SEAFARING SIGNS.

Sailors consider it ominous to whistle on shipboard, or carry a corpse in their vessel. Whistling at sea is supposed to cause increase of the wind, and is, therefore, much disliked by seamen, though sometimes they themselves practise it when there is a dead calm. The common sailors consider it very unlucky to lose a water-bucket or a mop. To throw a cat overboard, or drown one at sea, is the same. Children are deemed lucky to a ship, but clergymen and priests very unlucky.

To stumble and fall while going up the companion-way or in going aloft, is a sign that you will not get married during the year. If a man stumbles as soon as he comes on deck in the morning, it is a sign of ill-luck. The bottom of the foot itching is a sign that the person will walk on strange ground. A cat coming aboard a vessel betokens good luck. To first see a new moon over the left shoulder is a sign of bad luck, but over the right is good.

MADAME DE STAEL'S
BOOK OF NECROMANCY,

AND MANUAL OF

FORTUNE TELLING.

There are 8 hieroglyphics, containing 4 circles crossed over each other, and distinguished by their central figures, numbered from 1 to 8.

The person who intends to tell the Fortune of another by these Hieroglyphics, if a Female, for example, must first blindfold her, then lead her to the book opened in the middle of those pages containing the Hieroglyphics, and desire her to wish in her mind privately, and afterwards select by chance either one of the 8 pages of Hieroglyphics.

She must next point her finger to, and touch one of the circles in the chosen Hieroglyphic, containing a capital Roman Letter; after that operation unbandage her eyes, and show her the corresponding letter and its small number in the lines above, or below the same Hieroglyphic, against which is her fortune.

For amusement they can be cut into cards, and laid in a circle after shuffling, and answers may then be obtained by the same operations.

THE PERFECT FORTUNE TELLER.

1. Kindness unto your lover show,
   That lover you will wed I know.
2. Parted from friends you soon shall be,
   Marry and go across the sea.
3. Look for a letter with news strange,
   For the better your affairs will change.
4. Dream of wealth you may, dreams won't do,
   Hard work and poor fare are for you.

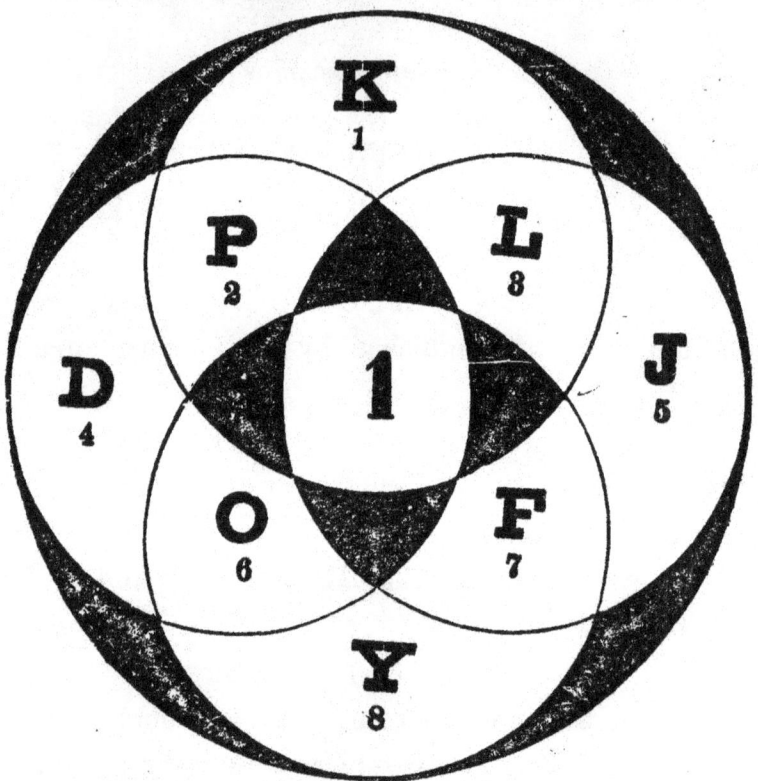

5. Jump for joy! you'll have a fair boy,
   Who'll plague you much—your life away.
6. Over the water you shall cross,
   Much wealth gain with a greater loss.
7. Fair is the partner you shall wed,
   Whose ways and temper I much dread.
8. You will lucky be at thirty,
   Bury one drunken and dirty.

9. Fortune on you now does not smile.
   But will bring you luck ere while.

10. Weddings three, in you house I see.
    For two sweet lasses and for thee.

11. Another lover you should seek,
    No more unto your false one speak.

12. There's a surprise; on you will call,
    Strangers whose news shall you appal.

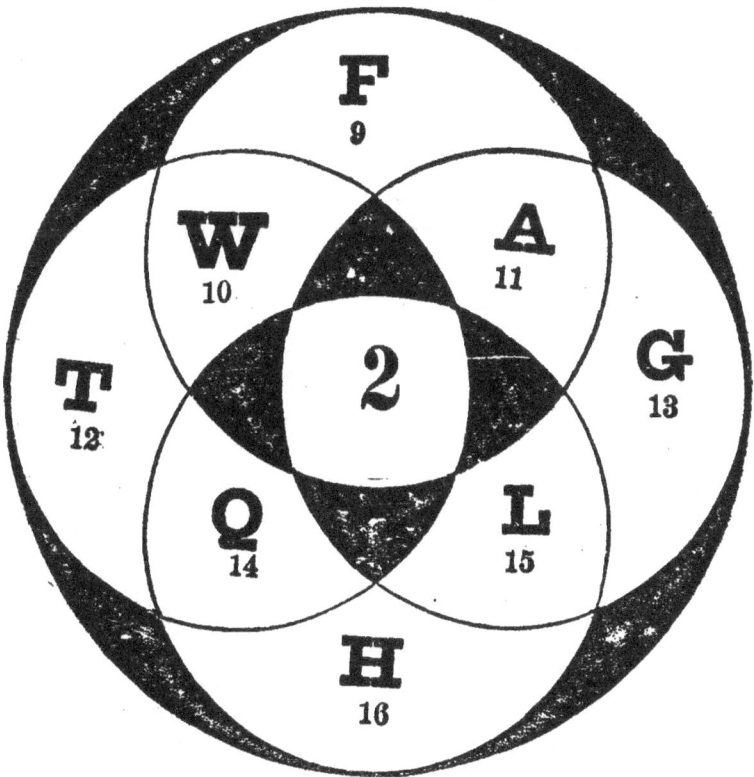

13. Great will be your consternation,
    Money lost must cause vexation.

14. Question not the decrees of fate!
    Death strikes the poor as well as great.

15. Life at present is hard with you
    Some better luck I see in view.

16. Husband or wife, if you draw this,
    Vexation and strife you scarce can miss.

17. United in wedlock you'll be,
    Have children, and grand-children three.

18. Before this year is well nigh o'er,
    Some property you'll gain at law.

19. Dark the spouse is you shall marry,
    Don't with your false fair one tarry.

20. Owls in search of prey, shun the light,
    Your owlish sweetheart walks at night.

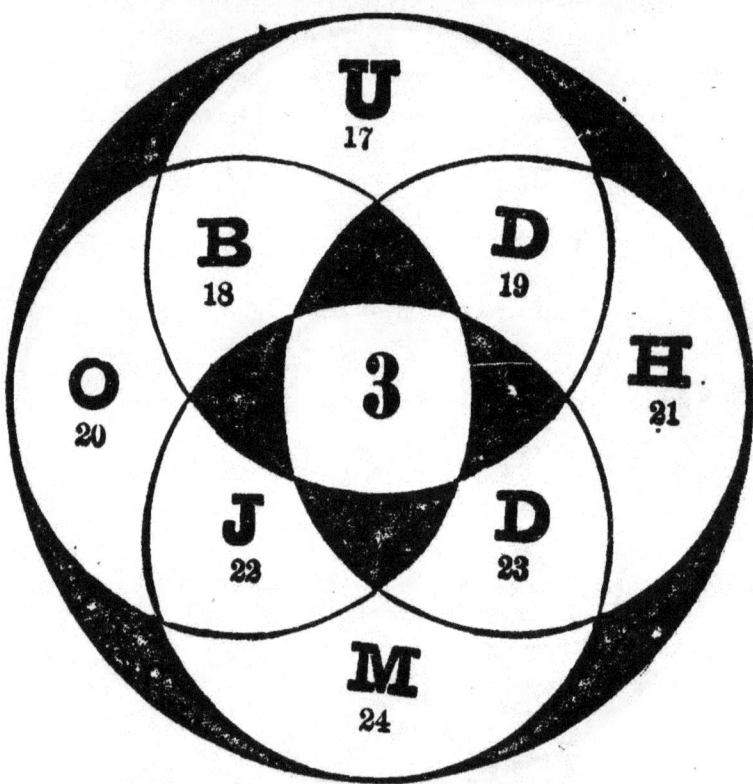

21. Husbands in plenty, wives many,
    Those who draw this get not any.

22. Jealousy so torments your mind,
    To be single you'd serve mankind.

23. Dangerous to travel; stay at home;
    In your own land you're doom'd to roam.

24. Many misfortunes you must see,
    But in middle-life fortunate be.

25. A relation leaves you by will,
    Money that shall your pockets fill.

26. Houses and lands, and gold in store,
    There's a time when you'll want no more.

27. Ever unfortunate and poor,
    You'll yet avoid the workhouse door.

28. Sing and laugh, that yet you may,
    Bad luck will make you weep some day.

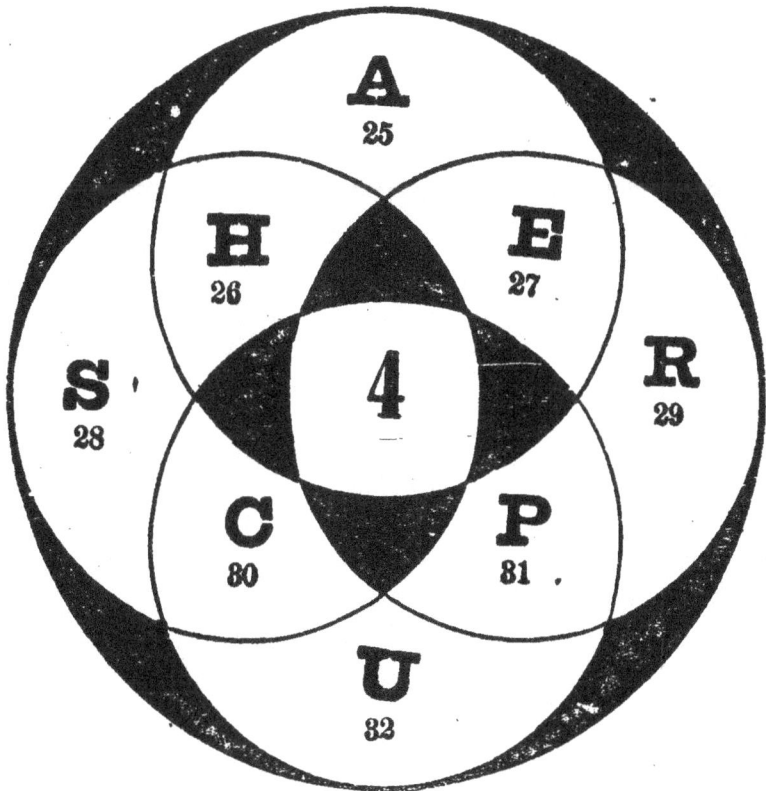

29. Rags for riches you shall exchange,
    A large house and park in which to range.

30. Children, many a partner cross,
    Is your sad lot with a heavy loss.

31. Prepare to change for the better,
    Some good news comes in a letter.

32. Under the mask of friendship's face,
    In your lover deceit I trace.

33. Blessings on you and yours shall shower,
    You'll rise to wealth, honor and power.
34. Letters will come with tidings great,
    Soon you alter your present state.
35. Quiet and humble your time will spend,
    In a cottage your life shall end.
36. Silver and gold by trade you'll earn,
    Yet all shall fail and your house burn.

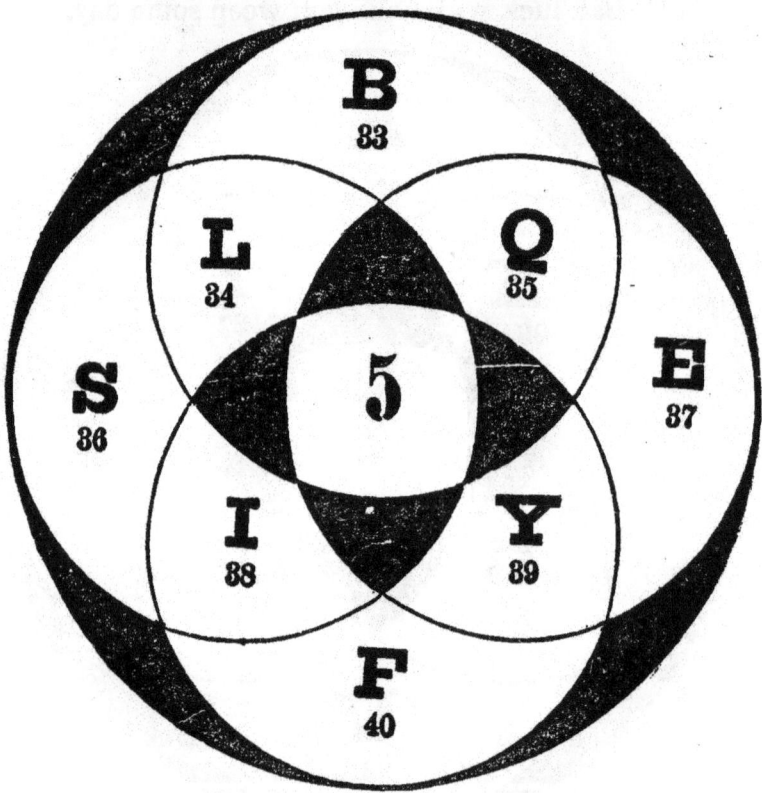

37. Enemies injure your good fame,
    Yet o'er them all shall shine your name.
38. In foreign lands you yet shall roam,
    Return with riches to your home.
39. You at this time are in great need,
    But shall emigrate and succeed
40. Fair and fat is the one you'll wed
    But will soon wish that one was dead.

THE PERFECT FORTUNE TELLER.

41. Wait, my dear, for a little while,
    Good Dame Fortune on you shall smile.

42. Now I can hear a parting breath,
    In your family there will be a death.

43. Kings shall ennoble your family,
    And Queens improve your destiny.

44. Endure, sweet love, your single state,
    Soon you shall wed a loving mate.

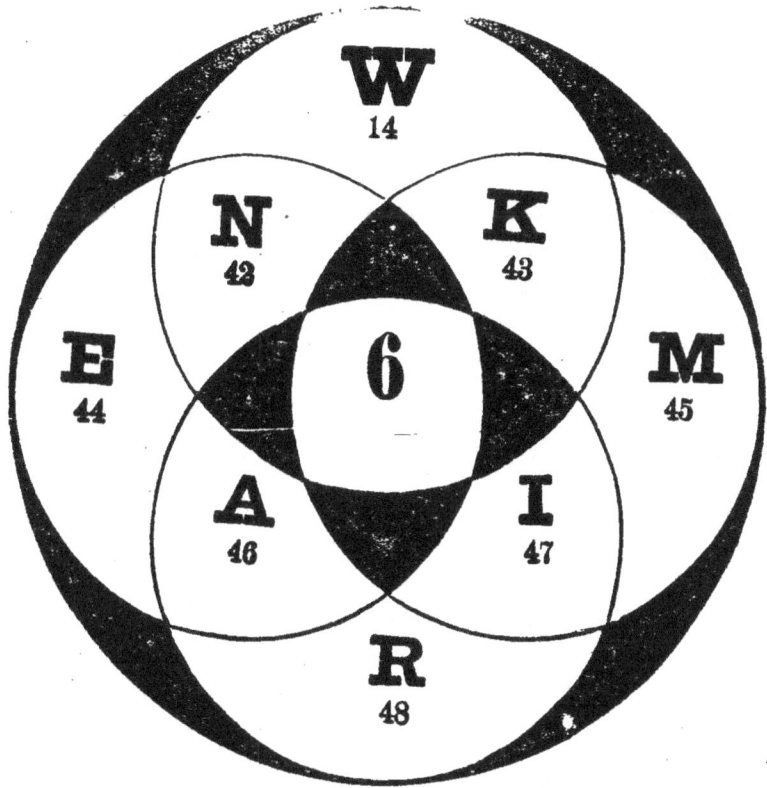

45. Marry you shall a cross fool,
    Who will starve you on water gruel.

46. A lazy, drunken sot, you'll wed,
    Though you may wish your first one dead

47. In after life look for things strange,
    For the better your luck shall change.

48. Roam you shall in Australia's clime,
    There live to see a better time.

49. Quickly prepare to change your state,
    You'll wed a poor hardworking mate.

50. On a ship's deck some night you'll stand,
    And be half-drown'd ere you reach land.

51. Houses you'll win, and lose by law,
    At one time rich, then rich no more.

52. Vexed oft you are, vexed more you'll be,
    Misfortunes are marked out for thee.

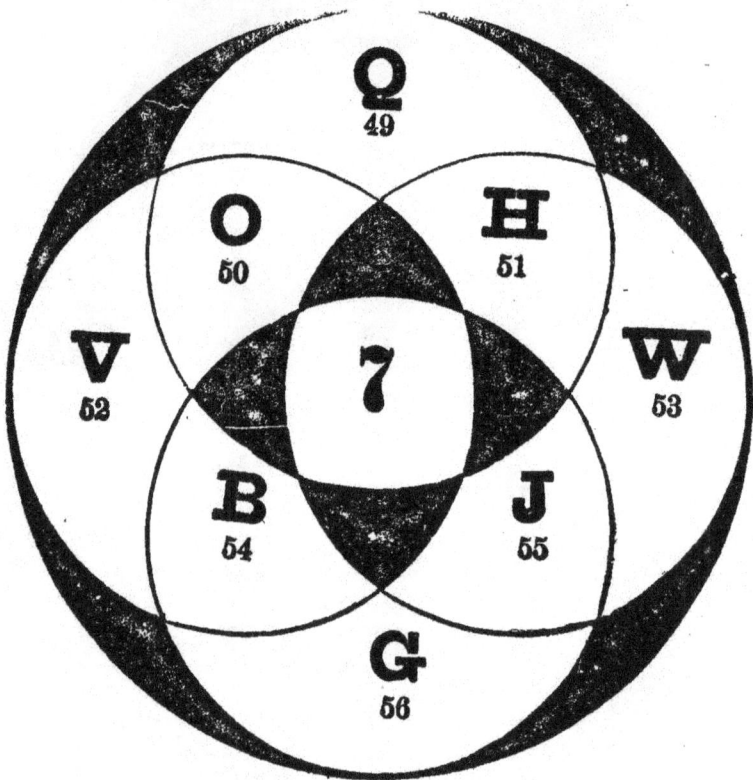

53. Want shall many years at you stare,
    At last you'll get a fortune fair.

54. Boys ten, and girls eight, are your lot,
    You must work hard to boil the pot.

55. Just as you're married you shall see,
    A will that must change your destiny.

56. Great will be your surprise ere long,
    A supposed friend has done you wrong.

57. Riches you wish for but too soon,
    You were born with a wooden spoon.

58. Changed for the worst is now your fate,
    'Twill change for better before late.

59. Ever unlucky for some years,
    Luck at 40 shall dry your tears.

60. Now to foreign climes emigrate,
    In that land you'll better your fate.

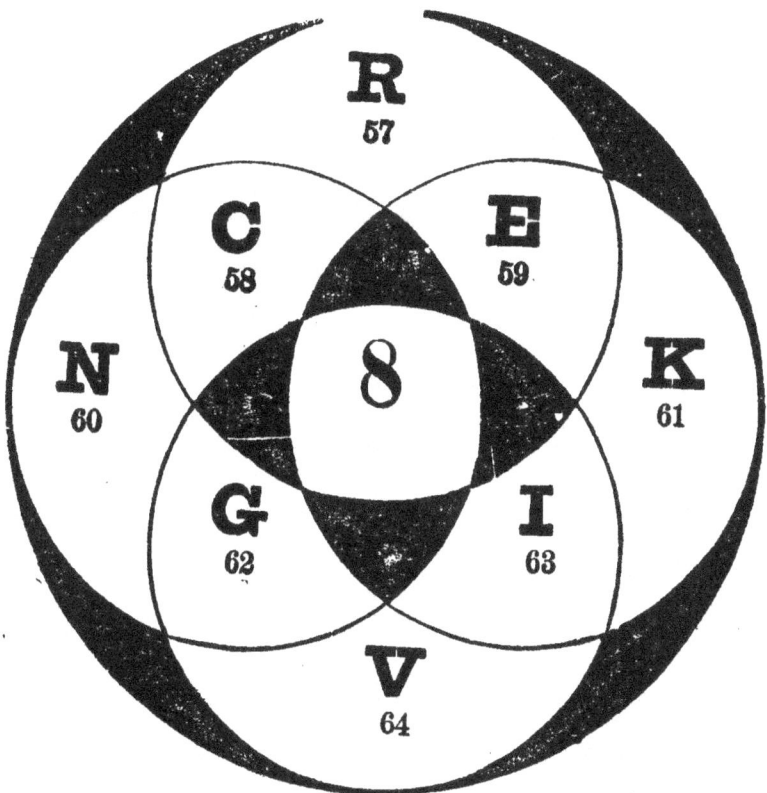

61. Kneel you shall at the altar's shrine,
    And wed a wealthy person fine.

62. Great deal of trouble you'll endure,
    'Tis your lot to be very poor.

63. In a short time news will surprise,
    And money brighten up your eyes.

64. Vineyards have grapes sour for your taste,
    The sweets of fortune you shall waste.

HINTS TO YOUNG LADIES

TO TRACE

THE MIND TO OUTWARD SIGNS.

If the man you contemplate have thick red lips, he will be simple, good natured and easily managed.

If he speak quick but distinct, and walk firm but erect, he will be ambitious, active, and probably a good husband.

If he blush, it is a favorable sign; but speaking bluntly and positively betokens much of headstrong self-will.

If he lose at cards snappishly, he is impatient; and to cheat at play for gain shows a mind unworthy of trust.

If he boasts of a lady's favors, he is to be avoided.

If he look pale in a passion, with pale lips, he cannot have either true love or real courage to defend you.

If he have a manly dark beard, or a handsome nose, he will be furnished with good qualities and abilities to please.

If he be of a yellow complexion, it implies moroseness and jealousy; if he have a pug nose, snappishness and vulgarity.

If he be beetle-browed, it shows duplicity and fickelness.

If he have a dimple on the cheek or chin, he will be the father of a handsome race, and generous.

If he truly love the woman he addresses, he will keep himself chaste and unspotted from the world.

THE
Signification of Dreams,
EXPRESSED IN NUMBERS.

Acquaintance.—Dreaming you fight them, signifies distraction, especially if the person dreaming is sick.   1, 11, 36

Ague.—Dreaming that you have one, shows an inclination to strong drink, spices, and other hot things.   3, 4, 15

Air.—To dream you see it clear and serene, shows you will be beloved and esteemed by all people, and that you shall be reconciled to all. But to dream that the air is dark, cloudy, and troubled, denotes sadness and sickness.   7, 8, 65

Alms.—To dream that they are begged of you, and you deny them shows want and misery to the dreamer; but to dream you give them freely is a sign of joy and long life.   23, 26, 28

Anchor.—Dreaming you see one signifies great assurance, and certain hope to all men.   12, 13, 23

Anger.—To dream that you have been provoked to anger, shows that you have many very powerful enemies.   16, 18, 26

Ants.—Dreaming of them shows an earthly, covetous mind.   9, 27, 31

THE PERFECT FORTUNE TELLER.

Apparel—Dreaming your apparel is proper, denotes prosperity and happiness.   4, 14, 24

To dream of white apparel is good only for priests. For the sick to dream of white apparel denotes death.   9, 33, 55

To dream of black apparel signifies the recovery of the sick   8, 17, 31

For rich men and servants to dream of being arrayed in scarlet robes is a signification of honor and liberty.   15, 25, 32

Apples.—To dream you see and eat sweet, ripe apples denotes joy.   7, 18, 21

To dream of sour apples signifies contention and strife.   17, 23, 31

Ass.—To dream you see an ass is a sign of malice. To dream you hear an ass bray shows you will meet with some loss. To see an ass run denotes trouble and misfortune.   4, 7, 12

Back.—To dream you see your back betokens some unhappiness. To dream your back is broken shows your enemies shall get the better of you. To dream of the backbone signifies health and joy.   1, 5, 9

Bagpipes.—To dream you play them denotes a great deal of trouble.   13, 21, 65

Banquet.—To dream of a feast is good and prosperous.   16, 19, 22

Barley Bread.—To dream you eat it betokens long life and health.   11, 13, 15

Barn.—Dreaming you see a barn stored with corn shows you shall marry rich.   4, 24, 52

Bathing.—Dreaming of a bath, and the water appearing clear, you are sure to prosper.   17, 19, 40

Beans.—Dreaming of eating beans betokens ill-health and trouble.   4, 15, 24

Bear.—To dream you see an old bear denotes you have a rich enemy.   2, 5, 9

Bees.—Dreaming that bees alight on you, and do you no injury, you will be carressed by worthy characters, if they sting you and then fly away, it bodes a momentary injury.   12, 17, 46

Beheading.—To dream that one has been beheaded, and that the head is separated from the body, denotes liberty to the prisoner, comfort to those in distress, health to the sick, and to creditors, payment of debts.   8, 17, 35

Belly.—To dream one one's belly is bigger and fuller than ordinary, shows his family and estate will increase proportionably. according to the greatness of his belly.   10, 30, 63

Birds.—Dreaming that you catch birds is a sign of profit, and to hear birds sing, is joy and delight.   55, 57, 60

Blindness.—To dream you are blind, denotes poverty.   4, 6, 9

Blackbird.—To dream you see and hear a blackbird and thrush singing upon the same tree, shows a female will have two husbands, and a male two wives.   6, 13, 65

Blood.—To dream you vomit much blood, and of a good color, is good for he that is poor, to dream you vomit corrupt blood is sickness to all.   2, 5, 9

Boat.—To dream that you are in a boat upon a river, lake, or pond of clear water, indicates joy, but if the weather be rough and tempestuous, the contrary.   12, 19, 64

Bridge.—For one to dream he goes over a broken bridge, signifies obstruction to business.   8, 16, 31

Butchers.—To dream of seeing butchers, is in general an unlucky omen, for it foretells some injury to the dreamer.   4, 11, 68

Cage.—To dream that a maid lets a bird out of a cage is a sign she will not keep her honor long, but will part with it as soon as she can.   19, 28, 36

Candle.—To dream you see a candle extinguished, denotes sadness, sickness, and poverty; to dream you see a shining lighted candle, is good to the sick, to dream you make candles, is a sign of rejoicing, to dream you see unlighted candles, shows you will have a reward for something you have done.   8, 16, 54

Cards.—To dream you play at cards, tables, or any other game, shows the party shall be very fortunate.   63, 64, 65

Carrots.—To dream of carrots, denotes profit.   16, 58, 60

Cart.—To dream of being tied in a cart, to draw like a horse or an ass, denotes servitude and pain to everybody, to dream that you are carried in your coach or cart, signifies to have might and authority.   7, 9, 11

Cattle.—To dream of keeping cattle, portends disgrace and loss to the rich, but profit to the poor, to dream of fat cattle, shows a fruitful year, but lean cattle, a scarcity.   16, 25, 57

Cheese.—To dream you eat cheese, is a sign of profit.   5, 13, 26

Children.—To dream that a man sees two or three children born, shows he shall have cause of joy. It is better to dream that you see boys than girls.   8, 12, 26

Clock.—To dream the clock strikes, and that you count, but that instant it stands still, forebodes death to some old friend, but if the hand moves again, the party will recover.   4, 17, 27

Clothes.—If a man dreams he has a new suit of clothes, it is a sign of honor. But to dream that you see your clothes burned, denotes loss and damage. Dreaming you see yourself dressed in black clothes, denotes joy   16, 18, 28

Clouds.—To dream of white clouds, is a sign of prosperity, clouds mounting high from the earth, denotes voyages and return to the absent and revealing of secrets. Clouds red and inflamed, show an ill issue of affairs; to dream of smoky, or obscure clouds, shows an ill time, or anger   19, 22, 46

Coach.—To dream of a coach drawn by four horses, and that the dreamer is delighted with the jaunt, either he or she may expect something will transpire to give joy and satisfaction in a month after.   23, 42, 64

Coals.—To dream you see dead coal, signifies expedition in business, to dream you see burning coals, threatens you with shame and reproach.   7, 16, 28

Coal-pit.—To dream of being at the bottom of coal-pits, indicates a match with a widow.   9, 25, 53

Cucumber.—Dreaming of eating cucumbers, denotes vain hopes, but to the sick it is a prognostic of recovery.   8, 19, 23

Dancing.—To dream that you see yourself dance, is good, but to him that is sick, or has any disease, it is evil.   6, 17, 22

Dark.—If one dream of being in the dark, and that he cannot find his way, denotes that the party so dreaming, shall be blinded with some passion, and much troubled.   14, 39, 50

Death.—Dreaming of death, signifies a wedding. For the sick to dream they are married, or that they celebrate the wedding, betokens death, or separation from her or his companions, friends, or parents.   15, 30, 44

Devil.—Dreaming that one has seen the devil, and is tormented, or otherwise very much terrified, is a sign the dreamer is in danger of being checked and punished by his sovereign prince or some magistrate.   5, 37, 43

Digging.—Dreaming you are digging is good, but to dream that your spades, or digging tools seem to be lost, it portends loss of labor, dearth of corn, or an ill harvest.   18, 29, 41

Ditch.—Dreaming you see great ditches or precipices, and that you fall into them, shows that you will suffer much injury, and your goods be in danger by fire.   4, 11 44

Dogs.—To dream of such dogs as belong to us, signify fidelity, but to dream of those which belong to strangers, means infamous enemies. Dreaming that a dog barks and tears our garments, betokens some endeavoring to deprive us of our livelihood.   7, 9, 28

Drinking.—Dreaming you are drinking when you are very dry, is a sure sign of sickness.   19, 21, 40

Eagle.—Dreaming you see an eagle in some high place is a good sign. If one dreams that an eagle lights upon his head, it betokens his death.   6, 14, 21

Earth.—To dream that a man hath good lands, or earth well enclosed bestowed upon him, with pleasant pastures, he will have a fine wife. If you dream you see the earth black, it betokens sorrow.   43, 45, 64

Eclipse.—If one dream that he sees the sun eclipsed it signifies the loss of his father, but if he sees the moon eclipsed in his dream, it foretels the death of his mother, but if the dreamer have neither father nor mother, then the death of the next nearest relation.   8, 11, 64

Elephant.—To dream of elephants is very favorable, and denotes riches and sagacity.   9, 12, 18

Evil Spirit.—Dreaming you see an evil spirit of a hideous physiognomy, shows that things will be revealed to you.   19, 22, 61

Eyes.—If you dream you have lost your eyes, shows you will violate your word, or else you or some of your children is in danger of death.   7, 25, 36

Eye Brow.—Dreaming your eyebrows are hairy, and of a good grace, is good, especially to women. But the eye brows without hair, shows she will be afraid to marry.   13, 15, 42

Earth-worm —Dreaming of earth-worms betokens secret enemies that endeavor to ruin and destroy us.   7, 11, 14

Face.—Dreaming you see a smiling face and countenance is a sign of joy. Dreaming you see a meagre, pale face, is a sign of trouble. Dream one washes his face, implies repentance for sin, a black face denotes long life.   28, 35, 55

Fall.—Dreaming you had a fall from a tree, and scratched by thorns, signifies you shall lose your office.   32, 44, 53

Father-in-law.—To dream one sees his father-in-law, is ill, whether he is dead or alive.   13, 15, 17

Fairs.—Dreaming of going to fairs, foretells sudden loss.   4, 11, 44

Feet.—Dreaming that a man's feet are cut off, is a sign of damage. Dreaming one hath a wooden leg, implies alteration of your condition, from good to bad. Dreaming you walk when your feet are sore is a token of fastening.   2, 15, 22

Fields.—To dream of fields and pleasant places, shows to a man that he will have a discreet and chaste wife, and to a woman a loving and prudent husband.   15, 21, 64

Fingers.—To dream you cut your fingers, or see them cut by another, betokens damage.   8, 13, 22

Fire.—For a married person to dream that the fire burns clear, and the smoke spins from the chimney, is a good omen, but to dream that the fire is difficult to light, and the smoke returns to the ground, is a sign that matrimony will prove incomplete. If the fire ceases to burn, it is a sign of separation.   3, 7, 19

Fish.—To dream you see or catch large fish, it is a token of profit. A woman with child to dream she is brought to bed of a fish, shows that she will be delivered of a dead child.   23, 41, 62

Flesh.—If any one dream he has increased in flesh, he will gain wealth. On the contrary, to dream you have got thin, shows that you will become poor.   3, 6, 35

Funeral.—Dreaming one goes to the funeral of a friend is good, the dreamer will have money left him, or marry fortune.   7, 8, 16

Garden.—Dreaming you walk in a garden and gathering flowers, the party so dreaming is given to pride.   17, 22, 36

Geese.—If you dream of the cackling of geese, you will have an increase of business, and much profit.   4, 7, 6

Gibbet.—Dreaming you see a person suspended on a gibbet is a token of a hurt and heavy affliction.   15, 23, 36

Goat.—If you dream of goats, it betokens wealth.   15, 33, 36

God.—Dreaming you worship God, is good. If you dream you receive pure favors from him it shows health.   8, 11, 23

Ground.—To dream you fall on the ground betokens dishonor, scorn, scandal and shame.   23, 45, 57

Hail.—Dreaming you see it hail, denotes sorrow.   2, 4, 8

Hair.—For a man to dream his hair is long, like a woman's betokens cowardice, and that he will be deceived by a woman. If you dream you see a woman without hair, famine and sickness will surely come. If you see a man bald and without hair, it denotes the contrary.   22, 34, 45

Head.—Dreaming you have a great head, or a head bigger than ordinary, and highly raised, denotes dignity.   12, 23, 35

Heaven.—Dreaming of heaven and that you ascend up thither, is an indication of grandeur and glory.   21, 34, 52

Hen.—If you dream you hear hens cackle or that you catch them, denotes joy, to dream you see a hen with chickens means loss and damage; to see a hen lay eggs is gain.   34, 46, 53

Hills.—To dream you are traveling over hills, and wading through great difficulties, and meet with assistance on the way, shows that you shall have good counsel and overcome all your troubles.   10, 23, 47

Horses.—Dreaming you mount a horse, is a happy omen. Dreaming you ride on a tired horse shows you are in love.   34, 46, 49

House.—Dreaming you build a house denotes comfort.   23, 42, 53

Husbandry.—Dreaming of a plough, is good for marriage. Dreaming of the yoke is good, but not for servants.   24, 45, 56

Ice.—Denotes an abundant harvest but to merchants, and men of other employments, it threatens hinderance and delay in their business.   32, 43, 56

Images.—Dreaming you make images of men, portends you will soon marry, have many children very like yourself.   21, 42, 61

Inn.—If you dream of an inn, it prophecieth death to the sick. The innkeeper indicates the same as the inn.   23, 45, 52

Iron.—To dream you are hurt with any article made of iron or steel, implies that you will meet a loss.   21, 34, 53

Keys.—To dream you lose your keys denotes passion. A key seen in a dream, to him that would marry, denotes that he shall have a handsome wife and a maid.   34, 42, 51

King.—Dreaming you converse with a king denotes honor.   12, 13, 23

Knees.—To dream that your knees are strong and steady shows health and strength, but to dream they are weak the contrary. If it be a woman she will be ready to obey her husband, and be very careful to govern her family.   17, 18, 19

Knife.—To dream you bestow a knife upon any body denotes injustice or quarrelling.   15, 23, 57

Laurel.—To dream you see a laurel tree denotes pleasure, and if you be married, it betokens inheritance of possesions.   34, 43, 53

Letters.—Dreaming you learn letters, is good to the illiterate, and those who can read it forecells evil.   11, 21, 32

THE PERFECT FORTUNE TELLER.

Marriage.—To dream that you do the act of marriage denotes danger. Marriage is a token of the death of some friend or relative.   1, 12, 23

Measles.—If any one dream he hath the measles, it denotes wealth, but it shall be coupled with infamy.   15, 22, 34

Milk.—To dream you drink milk is a very good omen.   9, 12, 15

Monkey.—To dream of monkeys shows you have strange, malicious, or secret enemies.   23, 34, 46

Moon.—To dream of the moon, is a good omen; it denotes sudden and unexpected joy, great success in love, and that the dreamer is tenderly adored. To dream of seeing the new moon is good for all.   20, 30, 40

Mouth.—If one dreams that his mouth is wider than ordinary, his family will be enriched, and he be more opulent than formerly. To dream that one's mouth is closed, and shut in such a manner that he cannot eat is a token of sudden death.   2, 5, 8

Music.—To dream you hear melodious music implies that you will hear some very acceptable news.   6, 9, 20

Nails.—To dream that one's nails are longer than usual, is a token of profit; and the contrary, of loss and discontent.   10, 20, 30

Night-mare.—For a woman to dream she is ridden by the night-mare shows she will be suddenly married; if a man, that he will be domineered over by a fool.   13, 22, 50

Nose.—To dream one has a fair and fine nose, is benefit to all. But to dream one has no nose, means the contrary; and to a sick man death. If any one dreams his nose has increased in size, he will become rich.   32, 40, 56

Oak.—To dream one sees a majestic oak, is a token of riches and profit to the dreamer or his friends.   2, 5, 9

Oil.—To dream that one anointed with oil is beneficial for a women, but for men it is ill.   21, 31, 41

Olive Tree.—Dreaming you see an olive tree denotes peace, delight, concord, and fruition of his desires.   42, 54, 61

Oranges.—To dream that one sees and eats oranges implies wounds, sorrow, and vexation.   11, 44, 50

Owls.—To dream of owls, betokens much melancholy.   23, 34, 45

Oysters.—To dream you are eating oysters is favorable.   17, 49, 51

Paper.—To dream you write on or read papers denotes news, to dream you blot or tear your paper, indicates the well ordering of business.   27, 31, 40

Paths.—Dreaming one walks in large plain or easy paths, betokens health, paths narrow or crooked, the contrary.   16, 27, 39

Peacock.—To dream you see a peacock, shows you will grow rich, and be in great honor   33, 44, 55

Peas.—Dreaming of peas well boiled, denotes success.   1, 4, 8

Pigeons.—To dream you see pigeons is a good sign, to dream that you see pigeons flying, denotes hearty news.   11, 16, 28

Pit.—To dream you fall into a pit, and cannot get out easily, denotes some serious calamity; to the sailor ship-wreck; to the farmer a bad harvest. But to dream you fall into a pit and cannot get out by any means, augurs death.   41, 45, 61

Prayers—To dream of praying is good, it shows future joy.   15, 21, 42

Quagmire.—Dreaming one has fallen into a quagmire, show they shall be very difficult to overcome or conquer.   10, 11, 44

Quarrels.—If a man dream of quarrels and fighting, he shall hear of some unlooked for news of women, or embrace some joy he thought not of.   4, 11, 44

Quince.—To dream one sees quinces, shows that they shall meet with some changes in their affairs, which shall be for the better.   5, 12, 13

Radishes.—To dream one eats or smells of radishes, signifies a discovery of hidden secrets and domestic jars.   22, 25, 27

Rainbow.—To dream you are reading romances, comedies or diverting books, signifies joy and comfort.   33, 41, 52

Rice—To dream of eating rice denotes obstructions.   15, 28, 31

Ride.—To dream you ride wito a company of men, is very lucky, but with women, misfortune and deceit.   8, 22, 32

Rings.—To dream you see a ring on the finger of any one, shows damage. To dream of plain gold rings, a wedding.   33, 45, 51

River.—To dream you see a river of water, clear and calm, is good; but should it appear disturbed or muddy, the contrary.   7, 42, 61

Roses.—To dream you see roses, is a sign of joy.   5, 11, 13

Rinsing.—To dream you rinse washed linen, is a sure sign of changing places.   25, 46, 63

Saddle.—To dream you were riding a horse without a saddle signifies poverty, disgrace and shame.   12, 32, 45

Sea.—To dream of walking upon the sea is good to him who would travel.   10, 11, 32

Serpent.—To dream you see a serpent turning and winding himself, signifies danger and imprisonment.   1, 5, 9

Shipwreck.—To dream you see a shipwreck, is most dangerous to all, except to those who are detained by force.   11, 34, 36

Shower.—If one dreams he sees a soft shower, without storm, tempest, or wind, it signifies gain, continued heavy rains, denotes quarrels.   13, 14, 21

Singing.—If any one dreams he sings, it signifies he will be affected and weep; to dream you hear singing or playing in concert upon instruments, signifies consolation.   33, 44, 55

Snow.—To dream you see the ground covered with snow, or that it is snowing, is favorable.   23, 43, 54

Tapestry.—To dream that one makes tapestry, denotes treachery and deceit. If you dream you buy curtains, drapery, &c., it foretells false acquaintance.   11, 22, 33

Tavern.—To dream you are in a tavern feasting with a party of friends, signifies joy and content.   32, 53, 65

Tempest.—To dream of great and long continuing tempests, signifies affliction and troubles.   9, 11, 22

Thunder.—Dreaming of thunder, signifies affliction to the rich, but to the poor it denotes, repose.   21, 33, 49

Torch.—When you dream in the night, that you hold a burning torch in your hand, it is a good sign.   1, 3, 5

Treasure.—To dream you find treasure in the earth is evil.   14, 26, 29

Trumpet.—Dreaming you hear a trumpet is good.   4, 7, 9

Tail.—To Dream you wear a tail, signifies profit, but to see animals with tails, such as monkeys or apes, shows abundance of company or amusements.   13, 35, 53

Velvet.—If you dream you trade with a stranger in velvet and other fine silks, it is profit and joy; to dream you see a person make velvet it indicates an industrious helpmate.   22, 34, 56

Victuals.—If you dream of victuals, and that you eat a variety of sorts, denotes loss, to dream you are in want of food is a token of pain.   33, 55, 59

Vinegar.—If you dream that you drink or make vinegar it betokens sickness, and sometimes death.   26, 35, 55

Virgin.—If you dream you discourse with the Virgin Mary, it betokens joy and consolation.   17, 22, 36

Veal.—If you dream that you eat veal or pork, it shows sickness or poverty. 32, 42, 61

Villain.—To dream you come in contact with a villain signifies that you are in danger of losing property. 19, 28, 34

Warts.—If you dream of having warts in the summer season, it is good to all persons. If the dream be in the cold or winter season, it shows the contrary. Also to dream of corns indicates the same. 31, 57, 61

Walnuts.—If you dream you see or eat walnuts, or hazlenuts, denotes difficulty and trouble, pickled walnuts, or in short pickles of any description, shows pains or vexations. 34, 54, 64

Washing.—For a man to dream that he washes or bathes himself in baths or hot houses, implies riches, prosperity, and health to the sick; that you see a woman washing, shows weakness. 12, 21, 31

Weasel.—If you dream of weasels, it shows some ill-natured woman by whom you will be ensnared. 16, 21, 45

Weddings.—For a man to dream of wedding a maid, who is himself sick, shows that he shall die quickly. If any one dream he is wedded to a woman that is deformed, it indicates discontent; if to a handsome woman, it denotes joy and profit. 14, 22, 35

Wife.—If a man dreams he sees his wife married to another, it betokens change of affairs, or else separation. If a man's wife dream that she is married to any other person than her own husband, she will be suddenly parted from him, or see him dead. 34, 42, 51

Wine.—Dreaming you drink white wine betokens peace, concord and happiness. Red wine denotes disputes and quarrels between friends. 15, 23, 36

Wood.—If you dream you saw or chop wood, it indicates to the poor, prosperity and content; but to the rich it shows poverty and loss. 11, 33, 51

Water.—To dream one sees clear running water is an indication that you will hear news from abroad. 16, 21, 39

Whitewash.—To dream you see a freshly whitewashed wall is an indication that you will be well thought of.   5, 14, 23

Young.—To dream that you are young signifies that you will have joy and happiness.   21, 32, 45

Yeast.—Dreaming that you purchase yeast, and afterwards make no use of it, betokens that you will be deceived by some friend, and meet with heavy losses in a pecuniary way.   33, 46, 53

Yew.—To dream that you see a yew-tree generally portends sickness and death to young people, but the reverse to those who are aged.   4, 19, 44

HYMEN'S LOTTERY.

Let each one present deposit any sum agreed on, but of course some trifle; put a complete pack of fifty-two cards, well shuffled, in a bag or reticule. Let the party stand in a circle, and, the bag being handed around, each draw three cards. Pairs of any are favorable omens of some good fortune about to occur to the party, and gets back from the pool the sum that each agreed to pay. The king of hearts is here made the god of love, and claims double, and gives a faithful swain to the fair one who has the good fortune to draw him; if Venus, the queen of hearts, it is the conquering prize, and clears the pool; fives and nines are reckoned crosses and misfortunes, and pay a forfeit of the sum agreed on to the pool, besides the usual stipend at each new game; three nines at one draw shows the lady will be an old maid; three fives, a bad husband.

72
76
414
16
8
73
45
57
29
27
17
51
4
90
958
84
22
39
87
75
77
68
96
12
10
55
40
82
38
21
31
106
36
98
525
64
58
44
70
100
7454
12
48
69

41
113
37
85
49
111
56
21
13
29
109
3
108
115
FEB
88
15
92
99
MAR
95
25
91
28
6
43
9
60
104
APR
32
66
122
116
26
83
19
65
67
SEP
112
AUG
42
23
86
120
52
46
59
11
OCT
2
17
103
NOV
118
DEC
74
81
71
14
119
63
53
97
35

MADAME AUBREY'S PALMISTRY.

OPERATIONS WITH THE MAGIC NUMBERS AND THE HAND OF DESTINY, WITHIN OR WITHOUT THE ORACULAR CIRCLE.

Stick a large pin in the middle* upright
In the midday sun, or midnight moonlight,
On a table, that the rays shine on it,
Then without mantle, cloak, shawl, or bonnet,
With your hair all flowing in locks, now mind,
Run fast round seven times, nor look behind;
Turn each time you pass Destiny's hand,
Blindfolded, for to learn a secret grand;
The seventh time the pin's shadow will show
Certain numbers, and all you wish to know,
Which you'll trace in a page coming after,
To make you weep, or force you to laughter.
These directions to a female I give,
May the fate I award, fit her to live.
Those males who are curious also to peep
At my Fortune Book, from maiden's must keep,
'Till whiskers and beard their manhood display,
Then to seek a wife and fortune they may.
Bandaged, without hat or coat they should run,
In the midnight moonlight, or midday sun,
Then the pin's shadow as I said before
Will show numbers, for which my book look o'er;
When, be it weal or woe, early or late,
Such will be your inevitable fate;
And should either of you wish for wedlock,
Blindfold well your eyes, and then three times knock.
On my *Oraculum,* and cross my palm
With gold or silver coin, to aid the charm;

---

*Just below the Number 83 at the joining of the middle fingers.

THE PERFECT FORTUNE TELLER.

On the eye and the heart it carefully place,
When your fortune now you may easily trace,
The number you chance to move the coin on,
Will tell you when you shall wed your loved one.

NOTE.—Within the brightest part of the Oracular Circle between and outside of the fingers, the fate told is the most propitious. In the darker parts of the Hand of Destiny, the answers denote luck of a mixed and variable kind. All the parts without the Oracular Circle are unfortunate. The three divisions between the joints of each finger correspond with the twelve months of the year, and when by the chance moving of the gold or silver money with which the palm of the Hand of Destiny is crossed, in the manner above indicated, it should stop on a particular month, that will denote the month of your marriage; and any number *below* thirty-two will indicate the day of the month it will be celebrated on. Where the line of the circle crosses through any portion of the light squares with figures on, being without as well as within the Circle, denotes a mixture of fortunate and unfortunate events. The dark squares are blanks. **The eye and the heart are the most fortunate of all.**

THE PERFECT FORTUNE TELLER.

THE EVENTS OF LIFE POINTED OUT BY THE HAND OF DESTINY.

56. Carriages, horses, houses, land,
    Shall be your fortune with things grand.

21. Proud lords shall be your serving men,
    And ladies wait upon you then.

13. Propitious shine your natal star,
    Riches you'll gain, and travel far.

3. Foreign countries shall see you oft,
   On beds of down you will lay soft.

108. Good news for you comes by the post,
     You'll get what you have lately lost.

15. Letters for you are on the road,
    Good luck I think they you forebode.

107. Property soon will come to you,
     At law you shall receive your due.

28. Money expected will arrive,
    You'll be fortunate if you strive.

6. Lawyers may vex you but will fail,
   The rights you gain will good entail.

61. A surprise awaits you ere long,
    With joy you'll sing a merry song.

83. A partner, ten children pretty,
    With a fine house in the city.

19. Unexpected wealth is your lot,
    In a foreign clime very hot.

1. A merchant, with plenty of gold,
   Shall marry you though rather old.

80. Ships, shops, and servants will be yours,
    Money you'll heap up by galores.

86. Plenty of stock, a country farm,
    To your life shall add quite a charm.

THE PERFECT FORTUNE TELLER.

59. A country house, and gardens fine,
    You shall enjoy and pass your time.

11. From abroad a friend shall send you,
    Welcome news that he has prov'd true.

2. A dark person bears a good heart,
   Whom with wealth you'll wed and ne'er part.

17. A letter and surprise are near,
    And both will make you happy dear.

81. A fair true friend loves you so well,
    Lots of wealth in your lap he'll tell.

71. A rich person will you marry,
    Take you off, and never tarry.

14. A lost friend for you shall be found,
    Who'll give you joy all the year round.

10. Houses and land I see in store,
    Titles and wealth, you'll want no more.

37. A fortune you'll enjoy awhile,
    Which by extravagance you'll spoil.

85. Riches you will some day acquire,—
    Lose it all, and no more aspire.

89. In business you will badly do,
    But much better luck awaits you.

30. You'll marry rich, at times live well,
    But poor you will become I tell.

33. You will life begin with bad luck.
    But better days will give you pluck.

110. A scold you'll wed, fond of noggins,
     Of gin, and giving you floggings.

119. A jealous, meanly-looking elf,
     Will starve you while he feeds himself.

97. Not very rich, or poor you'll be,
    Some day you shall cross o'er the sea.

THE PERFECT FORTUNE TELLER.

53. Poor awhile, before life's ended,
Your bad fortune shall be mended.

82. Bad news in a letter draws near,
And ominous to you I fear.

75. Your lover drinks so like a tippler,
Pray shun him or you'll never be richer.

47. A soldier handsome, fair and tall,
Very soon will to your lot fall.

111. A sailor from the briny main,
Will soon arrive to be your swain.

87. Married twice to country gabies,
Very poor and lots of babies.

40. The bride or bridegroom who draws this,
Shall have children and much bliss.

24. Look out, your swain is jilting you,
He hath half a dozen more it is true.

96. The day whereon you get married,
You'll wish at home you had tarried.

84. A loss of money here I see,
But much more is in store for thee.

90. 'Tis time your courting days were o'er,
For you'll see your lover no more.

31. Your sweetheart's false, choose another,
Better marry Old Nick's brother.

124. Though you'll not want, hard work's your lot,
And if you enlist you'll get shot.

22. An absent dear one from the wars,
Will soon arrive covered with scars.

29. A bank will break I fear ere long,
That will affect you through some wrong.

88. A will was made in your behalf,
News is coming to make you laugh.

THE PERFECT FORTUNE TELLER.

95. Death hovers here to give you life,
    Money has been left to your wife.

43. A lov'd one has troubles pass'd through,
    And from America shall send for you.

77. Expect news from the land of gold,
    You'll go there before you are old.

42. Australia is a land for thee,
    Emigrate there, and rich you'll be.

52. India's climes doth a letter send,
    It comes from a right valued friend.

46. A relation dies and leaves you
    Gold and silver coins, not a few.

23. This does a marriage betoken,
    Better had the ring been broken.

65. A large family with scanty crust,
    For to toil hard through life you must.

67. Lots of brats and a spendthrift spouse,
    Shall bring you yet to the workhouse.

26. Plodding in business up and down,
    You yet can never spare a crown.

32. Disastrous news comes o'er the sea,
    A shipwreck shall much concern thee.

66. Letters, a church, ring, and surprise,
    And news which shall open your eyes.

9. A stranger shall knock at your door,
    Whom you will wish to call no more.

25. You're building castles in the air,
    And always laughed at by the fair.

91. You think you love, and are lov'd too,
    No one with sound sense can you woo.

92. Failures in your trade I here see,
    But much better they soon shall be.

THE PERFECT FORTUNE TELLER.

99. An enemy strives to injure you,
But all your troubles you'll pass through.

115. A money-letter from a friend,
You'll receive before the month's end.

122. A wedding ring I see quite clear,
You will soon be married my dear.

116. Funerals in perspective I view,
Of those related near to you.

121. Your planet smiles on you benign,
Your number shows a lucky sign.

120. Though to-day you're filled with sorrow,
Luck shall fill your cup to-morrow.

114. Good fortune shall your prospects hail,
Although your present business fail.

112. Uphill and downhill trot through life,
On ill-fortune's nag without a wife.

103. Twice to church you shall smiling go,
First time for fortune, last for woe.

118. Your star in the ascendant is,
And your number denotes much bliss.

113. The herald of death cometh near,
Your family it concerns I fear.

41. A great fire and failure I see,
Unfortunate news comes to thee.

76. Trouble flieth on silent wings,
A note will tell you of bad things.

72. Law seemeth here to set his claws,
And sad news you'll hear from the wars.

16. Great disappointment now look for,
And in your affairs much uproar.

8. A little trouble forbodes you,
But you shall shortly it pass through.

THE PERFECT FORTUNE TELLER.

45. A birth will you much sorrow give,
But ends with good if it should live.

57 Secret malice doth you beset,
Prepare to break your enemy's net.

27. Money expected you have lost,
And sorrow it will yet you cost.

4. From the country you'll hear news **bad,**
But better comes to make you glad.

36. A partner falls to your lot,
Who by hard luck will skin the pot.

98. "Stich, stich, stich," is your sorry fate,
To fortune's cupboard you've come late.

64. Down down, down, you have ever gone,
You must live mean and your goods **pawn.**

58. Squalling children, a scolding wife,
And poor fare are yours through life.

70. Always dabble in soapsuds hot,
And wedded to a drunken sot.

100. In poverty must work fast your bones,
And of your "uncle" borrow loans.

74. For rich men's crumbs you'll always **scratch,**
And ever doomed old rags to patch.

12. Don't over your misfortunes whine,
I see a gleam of fortune shine.

48. For your own and your country's good,
You'll journey and work in a wood.

63. Lost property will cause vexation,
Taken by a man of station.

85. Mourn not, though just now your are **poor,**
Relief will soon enter your door.

94. You'll hate the time you e'er was **made,**
To marry a draggle-tail jade.

THE PERFECT FORTUNE TELLER.

105. A young man saileth o'er the sea,
Who will make love and marry thee.

69. Poor husbands and wives are well met,
One of such helpmates you will get.

54. I see strife and many crosses,
You will suffer heavy losses.

20. Your prospects at present looks well,
But ill luck's coming I can tell.

50. The sun shines cloudy on you now,
The moon reflects bad news I vow.

44. Grim poverty stares you in the face,
Future good for you I can trace.

5. Long and lazy, sallow and thin,
Is the one that will take you in.

93. Short and big-bellied regular sot,
Is the spouse that falls to your lot.

106. With sheepish face, a stupid calf,
Will be your future better half.

38. Nature's perfect caricature,
Will fall in love with you I'm sure.

55. Simplicity is so stamped on you,
To marry you a fool would do.

68. A dust-bin scraper doth you love,
Who lives just in the street above.

39. I fear this number denotes rags,
You'll wed a carrier of bones in bags.

18. Of coach, servants, and money dream,
For that is all you'll get I ween.

78. A ragged fortune is your store,
Work hard you may make it worth more.

51. Good men are disposed of they say,
A *tenth of one* you marry may.

THE PERFECT FORTUNE TELLER.

117. Comely, pretty, your sweetheart is,
Though poor, you will both reap **much bliss.**

7. Kind and gentle as a sweet dove,
Your humble swain is worth your love.

102. A train will shortly to town bring,
Some one who'll make you cry and **sing.**

73. Here's some sly kissing been going **on,**
Your swain you can't depend upon.

79. A nice baby elsewhere you hide,
And what secret does it betide?

49. Many boys and girls you shall have,
And you'll descend poor to the grave.

62. A law suit impends over you,
Pay if you can the debt that's due.

84. You will wed I see a short humpback'd **swain,**
But not my bell-ringer of Notre Dame;
Quasimodo I love, and he loves me,
By midnight, moonlight, in the old belfry.

THE ART

OF

FORTUNE TELLING BY CARDS.

Take a pack of Cards, shuffle and cut them three different times, lay them on a table, nine in a row; if a man he may choose one of the kings to represent himself; if a woman she must select one of the queens; then the queen of the chosen king, or the king of the chosen queen, will stand for a husband or wife, mistress or lover, of the party whose fortune is to be told; and the knave of the suit, of the most intimate person of their family; remember that every thing is within your circle as far as you count nine, any way from the card that represents the person, his wife, or her husband, and their intimate friend; also that the ninth card every way, is of the greatest consequence.

Ace of Clubs promises great wealth, much prosperity in life and tranquillity of mind.

King of Clubs announces a man who is humane, upright, affectionate and faithful in all his undertakings; he will be happy himself, and make his connections so if he can.

Queen of Clubs shows a tender, mild, and rather amorous disposition one who would probably yield her maiden person to a kind lover before the matrimonial knot be tied but they will be happy, love each other, and be married.

Knave of Clubs shows an open, sincere friend who will exert himself warmly in your interest and welfare.

THE PERFECT FORTUNE TELLER.

TEN OF CLUBS denotes that riches will come speedily from an unexpected quarter; it also threatens the loss of some dear friend.

NINE OF CLUBS shows that you will displease some of your friends by a too steady adherance to your own opinions.

EIGHT OF CLUBS shows the person to be covetous, and extremely found of money; that he will obtain it, but that it will rather prove a torment than a comfort to him, as he will not make a proper use of it.

SEVEN OF CLUBS promises the most brilliant fortune and the most exquisite bliss that this world can afford; but beware of the opposite sex, from these alone can you experience misfortunes.

SIX OF CLUBS shows you will enter into a very lucrative partnership, and that your children will behave well.

FIVE OF CLUBS declares that you will shortly be married to a person who will mend your circumstances.

FOUR OF CLUBS shows inconstancy for the sake of money and change of object.

TRAY OF CLUBS shows that you will be married three times, and each time to a wealthy person.

DEUCE OF CLUBS shows that there will be some unfortunate opposition to your favorite inclination, which will disturb you.

ACE OF DIAMONDS signifies a letter.

KING OF DIAMONDS shows a man of fiery temper, continued anger, seeking revenge, and obstinate in his resolutions.

QUEEN OF DIAMONDS signifies that the woman shall be fond of company, be a coquette and not be over virtuous.

KNAVE OF DIAMONDS however near related, will look more after his own interest than yours; he will be tenacious in his own opinion, and fly off if contradicted.

TEN OF DIAMONDS promises a country husband or wife, with great wealth and many children; the card next to it tells the number of children, it also signifies a purse of gold.

NINE OF DIAMONDS declares that the person will be of a roving disposition, never contented with his lot and for ever meeting vexations and disappointments.

EIGHT OF DIAMONDS shows that the person, in their youth will be an enemy to marriage, and thus run the risk of dying unmarried; but if they do marry it will be late in life, and then it will be with a person whose disposition in so ill assorted to theirs, that it will be the cause of misfortune.

SEVEN OF DIAMONDS shows you will be tormented by the infidelity of your conjugal partner, and waste of your goods.

SIX OF DIAMONDS shows an early marriage, and premature widowhood; but a second marriage will probably be worse.

FIVE OF DIAMONDS shows that you will have good children, who will keep you from grief.

FOUR OF DIAMONDS shows the inconstancy of the person you will be married to, and great vexation to yourself through the whole course of your life.

TRAY OF DIAMONDS shows that you will be concerned in quarrels, law suits and domestic disagreements; your partner for life will be of a vixinish and abusive temper, fail in the performance of the nuptial duties, and make you unhappy.

DEUCE OF DIAMONDS shows that your heart will be engaged in love at an early period, that your parents will not approve your choice, and that if you marry without their consent they will hardly forgive you.

ACE OF HEARTS signifies feasting and pleasure; if the ace is attended by spades, it fortels quarreling; if by hearts, it shows affection and friendship; if by diamonds, you will hear of some absent friend; if by clubs, merry making.

KING OF HEARTS shows a man of good-natured disposition but hot and rather hasty in his undertakings, and very amorous.

QUEEN OF HEARTS denotes a woman of fair complexion, faithful and affectionate.

KNAVE OF HEARTS is a person of no particular sex, but always the dearest friend or nearest relation of the consulting party. You must pay great attention to the cards that stand next to the knave, as from them alone you can judge whether the person it represents will favor your inclination or not.

TEN OF HEARTS shows good nature, and many children, it is a corrective of the bad tidings of the cards that stand next to it, and if its neighboring cards are of good import, it ascertains and confirms their value.

NINE OF HEARTS promises wealth, grandeur, and high esteem; if cards that are unfavorable stand near it, you must look for disappointments; and a reverse, if favorable cards follow; these last at a small distance, expect to retrieve your losses, whether of peace or of good.

EIGHT OF HEARTS is a sign of drinking and feasting.

SEVEN OF HEARTS shows the person to be fickle and of an unfaithful disposition; addicted to vice, inconstant, and subject to the mean art of recrimination to excuse themselves, although without foundation.

SIX OF HEARTS shows a generous, open and credulous disposition, easily imposed upon, ever the dupe of flatterers, but the good natured friend of the distressed. If this card comes before your king or queen, you will be the dupe; if after, you will have the better.

FIVE OF HEARTS shows a wavering and unsteady disposition, never true to one object, but free from any violent attachment.

FOUR OF HEARTS shows the person will not be marrried until very late in life, which will proceed from too great delicacy in making a choice.

TRAY OF HEARTS shows that your own imprudence will greatly contribute to your experiencing the ill-will of others.

DEUCE OF HEARTS shows that extraordinary success and good fortune will attend the person, though if unfavorable cards attend, this will be a long time delayed,

ACE OF SPADES totalty relates to affairs of love, without specifying whether lawful or unlawful; it also denotes death when the card is upside down.

THE PERFECT FORTUNE TELLER.

KING OF SPADES shows a man ambitious and sussessful at court, or with some great man who will have it in his power to advance him, but let him beware of a reverse.

QUEEN OF SPADES shows that a person will be corrupted by the rich of both sexes; if she is handsome a great attempt will be made on her virtue.

KNAVE OF SPADES shows a person who, although they have your welfare at heart, will be indolent to pursue it with zeal unless you frequently rouse their attention.

TEN OF SPADES is a card of bad import; it will in a great measure counteract the good effect of the card near you.

NINE OF SPADES is the worst card in the pack; it portends dangerous sickness, a total loss of fortune, cruel calamities, and endless dissention in your family.

EIGHT OF SPADES shows ou will experience strong opposition from your friends, or those you imagine to be such; if this card comes close to you, leave your plan and adopt another.

SEVEN OF SPADES shows the loss of a most valuable friend, whose death will plunge you in very great distress.

SIX OF SPADES announces a mediocrity of fortune and very great uncertainty in your undertakings.

FIVE OF SPADES will give very little interpretation of your success; it promises good-luck in the choice of your companion for life, that you will meet with one fond of you, and immoderately attached to the joys of Hymen; it shows your temper rather sullen.

FOUR OF SPADES shows speedy sickness, and that your friends will injure your fortune.

TRAY OF SPADES shows that you will be fortunate in marriage, but that your partner will be inconstant, and that you will be made unhappy thereby.

DEUCE OF SPADES always signifies a coffin, but who it is for, must depend entirely on the other cards that are near it.

ASTRAGALOMANCY.

Take two dice, marked as usual with the numbers 1, 2, 3, 4, 5, 6. Write the question upon a paper, which you pass through the smoke of frankincense. Place the paper reversed upon the table, in such a manner as to conceal that which you have written, then throw alternately one dice and two at a time. You write the letters in the manner they present themselves and you have the answer.

Here are the letters corresponding to the different numbers which can thus be obtained:

1	2	3	4	5	6	7	8	9	10	11	12
a	e	i	o	u	b	c	d	f	g	l	r
		y			p	k	t	s	j	m	
					v	g	x			n	
							z				

Often times initials only are obtained, then the intelligence of the seer will complete the word.

CANDLE OMENS.

If a candle burn blue, it is a sign that there is a spirit in the house, or not far from it. A collection of tallow, says Grose, rising up against the wick of a candle, is styled a winding sheet, and deemed an omen of death in the family.

A spark at the candle, denotes that the party opposite to it will shortly receive a letter. A kind of fungus in the candle, predicts the visit of a stranger from the part of the country nearest the object. Others say it implies the arrival of a parcel.

CAULS.

Cauls are little membranes found on some children, encompassing the head, when born. This is thought a good omen to the child itself, and many believe that whoever obtains it by purchase will be fortunate and escape dangers. The caul is esteemed an infallible preservative against drowning, and is much sought after by sailors.

JUDGMENTS DRAWN FROM THE MOON'S AGE.

1. A child born within twenty-four hours after the new moon will be fortunate and live to a good old age; whatever is dreamed on this day will be fortunate and pleasing to the dreamer, various undertakings will succeed if begun on this day.

2. The second day is very lucky for discovering things lost, or hidden treasure; the child born on this day will thrive, but the dreams are not to be depended upon.

3. A child born on this day will be fortunate through persons in power, and whatever is dreamed will prove true.

4. The fourth day is bad; persons failing on this day rarely recovery, and the dreams will have no effect.

5. This day is favorable to begin a good work, and the dreams will be tolerably successful; the child born on this day will be vain and deceitful.

6. The dreams of the sixth day will not immediately come to pass, and the child born will not live long.

7. Do not tell your dreams on this day, for much depends on secresy; if sickness bef ll you on this day, you will soon recover; the child born will live long, but have many troubles.

8. Dreams of the eighth day will come to pass; whatever business a person undertakes this day will prosper, and any thing that is lost will be found.

9. The ninth day differs very little from the former, the child born this day will acquire great riches and honor.

10. The tenth day is likely to be fatal; those who fall sick will very rarely recover; but the child born on this day will live long, and be a great traveler.

11. The child that is born on the eleventh day will be much

devoted to religion, and of an engaging form and manner; if a female she will possess an uncommon share of wisdom and learning; this day is good to begin a journey, to marry, or to engage in business.

12. Dreams on the twelfth day are rather fortunate, and the child born, will live long and be very sensible; yet a person who falls sick on this day will rarely recover.

13. Dreams on this day will prove true in a very short time

14. If you ask any one a favor on this day, it will be granted.

15. The sickness that befals a person on this day is likely to prove fatal; that which was lost yesterday may be found to-day.

16. The child that is born on the sixteenth day will be of very ill manners and unfortunate; it is, nevertheless, a good day for buying and selling all kinds of merchandise.

17. The child born on this day will be very foolish, it is an unfortunate day to contract marriage, or any kind of business.

18. The child born on this day will be very valiant, but will suffer considerable hardships; if a female, she will be chaste and industrious, and live respected to a great age.

19. This day is dangerous; the child born will be very ill-disposed and malicious; it is very unfavorable for dreams.

20. Dreams on this day are true; children born will be dishonest.

21. The twenty-first day, the dreams will be vain and untrue; the child born will grow up healthy and strong, but be of a selfish ungentle turn of mind.

22. The child born will be very fortunate, and will be of a cheerful countenance, religious, and much beloved; any kind of business begun on this day will be unfortunate.

23. The child born on this day will be of an ungovernable temper, forsake his friends, wander about in a foreign country, and be rather unhappy through life; it is a happy day to marry on, and all business begun on this day will be successful.

24. The child born on this day will achieve many heroic actions, and be admired for his extraordinary abilities.

25. The child born on this day will be wicked, will meet with many dangers, and come to an ill end; it is a very unfortunate day, and threatens every thing with disappointment and crosses; whoever falls sick on this day very seldom recovers.

26. Dreams on this day are certain, and the child then born will be greatly esteemed.

27. This day is very favorable for dreams, and the child born will be of a sweet and amiable disposition.

28. This day is bad for dreams, and whoever falls sick on it is in great danger; the child born on it will be its parents delight, but will not live to any great age.

29. This day is good for dreams, but children born on it will experience many hardships, though in the end they may turn out happily. It is good to begin business or marry on this day.

THE ABRACADABRA AMULET.

The most celebrated of amulets, to be worn upon the person and to which marvelous powers are attributed, is that which forms the word Abracadabra. It will cure many maladies, among others the fever, twice or thrice. But it is necessary that the letters be in a triangle, as follows:

```
ABRACADABRA
ABRACADABR
ABRACADAB
ABRACADA
ABRACAD
ABRACA
ABRAC
ABRA
ABR
AB
A
```

This mysterious triangle must be written upon a piece of square paper, which is then folded in such a manner as to conceal the triangle. A white thread, passed in the form of a cross, closes this amulet, which is suspended from the neck by a linen ribbon. After wearing it nine days, you go to the bank of a stream, whose course runs towards the setting sun. The amulet is thrown over the shoulder with the eyes closed, or without looking at it. The charm having operated, you should go home cured.

Amulets are likewise made with the Psalms of David.

Travellers, to avoid danger, carry the 16th psalm under the left armpit.

To preserve memory, the 18th is recited seven times over a glass of wine.

To be strong, the 70th psalm is written on a piece of bearskin and worn suspended from the neck.

To preserve one's self from the bite of rabid dogs you write upon a parchment the words: *Hax, pax, max,* and wear it near the liver.

The formula *Och! Och!* engraven with a diamond point upon brass, will drive away fleas and other vermin.

CALENDAR OF FATE;

OR,

THE INFLUENCE OF SAINT'S DAYS UPON THE AFFAIRS OF PERSONS BORN ON EITHER OF THE UERDERMENTIONED DAYS.

The reader is referred to any almanack for the dates of the undermentioned festivals and fasts.

EPIPHANY, OR TWELFTH DAY.

It is fortunate to be born on this day; you are sure to rise and prosper in life, especially after the twenty-fifth year of your age has elapsed. It is also a good day to commence any new trade, commerce, or speculation.

HILARY.

Gives fortune to women, the reverse to men.

SAINT PAUL.

If it rains or snows on this day, bread will be dear after the next harvest; the wind being high, betokens war to the nation; a storm, the death of a person high in power. This day is good to ask a favor on, or begin a land journey, but not a voyage.

ST. PETER.

Gives rise in life to the woman, the reverse to the man, and is generally bad to all affairs of importance; a building should not be commenced on this day.

THE PERFECT FORTUNE TELLER.

VIRGIN MARY.

Gives brave men and virtuous women many trials in life which their prudence will overcome, and give competence to their latter days. Good to ask favors on but not to write for them; also good to commence any large undertaking.

ST. SWITHIN.

Gives to either sex, once at least in the course of their lives, an opportunity to elevate them—happy they who seize it. It is a lucky day for cards to a young beginner, and lottery speculation, but not to favors, or commence a courtship, voyage, or journey.

ST. MATTHIAS.

Not fortunate for speculators, but good to begin a steady trade, apprentice a child on, or make an agrement. It is not favorable to make requests on, especially to borrow money.

DAVID.

A person born on this day will travel much and have fortunate chances, prosperity will depend much on the use he or she makes of these advantages. This is a lucky day to make loans on interest, or enter into any profitable speculations, but not to make wills or plant trees. Dreams on this night are sure to come to pass.

GREGORY.

Lucky to commence either a voyage or journey, yet those born on this day will meet many crosses and stumbling blocks in their pursuits of the capricious goddess Fortune.

MICHAEL.

Let those born on this day beware of entering into any conspicuous plot or meeting, let them be frank, open, and generous in their manners, content with their station, and faithful to those they are bound to serve, or they will have cause to repent; it is easier to avoid evil than depart from its path. This is a good day for any new undertaking.

DUNSTAN.

Write no love-letters on this day, but it is good to those in commerce or the common occurrences of life. Persons born on this day are not very fortunate in life, except those intended for the church, then their success is pre-eminent; it is also a good day to launch a ship on, or buy in stock.

THOMAS.

A bustling life, much industry, but some heavy losses about the meridian of life, which will be surmounted. A woman thus born is likely to become a widow, and an excellent one she will make for the benefit of her offspring—her children will indeed call her blessed. A good day for sea affairs.

CHRISTMAS DAY.

Gives a fortunate birth, though not generally shown in the first years of life.

ST. STEPHEN.

Gives a thorny path—the only hope is by the love and friendship of some persons of better destiny than yourself, particularly marriage. It is a good day to seek favors or recover lost property.

SYLVESTER.

Gives a love of change and blameable variety. A good day for marriage, contracts, and apprenticeships, but not for reconciling enemies.

ANCIENT METHOD OF AVERTING FROST.

The husbandman who desired that in their season his fruit trees should be laden with fruit, covered them with a band of straw on the night celebrated by the Polytheists as the renewing of the invincible sun; and in the Christian Church, as the coming of our Savior, the night when the sun, supposed to be enchained for ten days by the winter solstice, begins to arise again toward the equator, and on which we often find cold suddenly and intensely developed. Experience has proved that this precaution will effectually protect trees from the hurtful effects of frost.

In the eighth century, they hoped to avert hail and storms by pointing long poles toward the skies. This measure reminds us of what was recently proposed, and, fifty years ago, was accredited by Berthollon, the naturalist. But, as at the end of the poles just mentioned, pieces of paper inscribed with magical characters were affixed, the custom seemed to be tainted with sorcery, and was consequently proscribed by Charlemange.

The instruments called paragrandines were intended to avert hail storms, and according to Seignior Antonio Perotti and Dr. Astolfi, they have succeeded in averting hail as efficiently as conductors in obviating danger from lightning. Seignior Perotti reports that, having fixed up several of them on a piece of land containing sixteen thousand perches, both his corn and his vines were protected, although fourteen hail-storms had occurred in the current year, which did great mischief in the fields; and in an official notice to the government of Milan, by the gonfaloniere of St. Pietro, in Casale, a very favorable account, also, is given of these protectors from hail. They are formed of metallic points and straw ropes, bound together by hempen or flaxen threads.

The inhabitants of Cleone in the Argolide, imagined they could distinguish, from the appearance of the sky the approach of frost that would endanger their crops, and immediately they endeavored, by offering sacrifices to the gods, to avert the evil. Other nations sang sacred hymns for this purpose.

EXPERIMENTS

ON

FORTUNE AND DESTINY,

WITH

DOMINOES, CARDS AND DICE.

―――•―•―――

Let these amusing oracles be tried as soon after sunset as possible; not before, for it is unlucky; but no particular day is required or prohibited.

WITH DOMINOES.

Repeat a wish to yourself three times, have the dominoes in a large or small basket; draw one; if the number is a double one you will get your wish— an even one, such as six and four, or four and two, you are left in doubt— an odd and an even number together is fatal to success—double six in this trial is a capital prize, showing your wish will bring you happiness—double blank, the death of one near to you.

WITH DICE.

Cast three dice three times into a small circle chalked with your own hand, and surmounted with your Christian name in full length; if the whole product does not amount to forty-one, you will not get your wish. Ones and twos turning up in this experiment denote some trivial teazing vexations near at hand. The higher the number, the more prosperous to your felicity in respect to the wish in question. One of the dice rolling out of the circle shows the near approach of a calamity, in which you will be interested particularly.

ANOTHER.

To know if a journey, or indeed any undertaking on land, will be successful or answer the end required, cast two dice, well shaken, into the palm of your left hand, as it is placed for that purpose on a table. Exactly seven is a doubt; under seven, disappointment; the lower the number the worse; over seven and higher the better.

WITH CARDS.

Shuffle the cards three times, wishing the same wish each time, but if you are in company you need not repeat them aloud; cut the cards into seven divisions, face downwards; close your eyelids, and then take up the first parcel on which you place your hand. If it contains the nine of hearts, the ace of diamonds, the three of clubs, or any three cards of the same number or quality, you will have your wish completed; the more of these cards is the chosen number, the better to your advantage; none of them is a sure indication of disappointment, and the more the number of sable cards, in this respect, the more for your expectations of happiness.

ANOTHER METHOD.

Shuffle the cards well, but do not cut them; deal twenty-one off the top as you keep repeating your desire; shuffle these again, and cut them in three with their faces upwards. Aces in this case are reckoned not as ones; but the superior cards. Thus, if the three cards are all under seven, you will never get your wish; if all above seven, you will be certain of it. Some under and some over, a doubtful case; but two of them, bearing a majority, affords much hope. The three being sevens, which has happened, the very climax of prosperity. You will lead a gay life. Several diamonds in a group show prosperity.

ANOTHER.

If a servant wishes to know about the situation to which she is going, let her lay out the cards, first taking from the pack the twos, threes, fours, and sixes as useless; leave in the fives. Let the maiden choose one of the queens, as a representative of herself before she shuffle the cards; then cut them into three divisions, and, taking the middle, lay the cards out in a half circle, and face upwards on the table, and make the following

THE PERFECT FORTUNE TELLER.

> Good understanding and memory ruleth its fate,
> As a lover of truth happy will be its state.

LEO, from 23d July to 22d August, inclusive.—Children born under this sign have a strong inclination to justness; are lovers of piety and truth; and have honest, candid, and upright minds.

VIRGO, from 23d August to 22d September, inclusive.—Children born under this sign are clever, prudent, attentive, pious, sociable; and in company cheerful.

LIBRA, from 23d September to 23d October, inclusive.—Children under this sign are true-hearted, discreet, pious, solitary; and very beneficient to the poor; are lovers of justice, truth and candor.

SCORPIO, from 24th October to 21st November, inclusive.
> Scorpio, the Scorpion, truly is a vicious sign,
> Children born beneath her shade seldom brightly shine,
> Subtle, wrathful, revengeful, trouble do they give,
> Clandestinely, they'll seek their ends, long as they live.

SAGITARIUS, from 22d November to 21st December, inclusive.
> Sagitarius, the Archer, mixed kind of luck shows,
> All children born under it, much wealth ne'er shall know.
> Mild, kind, and intelligent, knowing how to buy and sell,
> They'll try to manage prudently, and to thrive well.

CAPRICORN, from 22d December to 19th January, inclusive.
> Capricorn, or the Goat, is another varied sign,
> Babes born beneath it with melancholy will whine,
> Wrathful may perhaps become, or penetrating,
> Now given to sadness, and then to deep thinking.

AQUARIUS, from 20th January to 18th February, inclusive.
> Aquarius, or the Waterman, shows wisdom sedate,
> Will be imbibed by children subject to its fate,
> Have a genius for study, and learning the law,
> Divinity or history, or else inclined to war.

PISCES, from the 19th February to 20th March, inclusive.
> Children born under it will be kind and clever,
> To serve the poor or strangers will be ready ever,
> May be fond of priests, and be duped by ice in the arts.
> So they'll require training to influence ined a most im-

SIGNS OF THE NAILS.

Broad Nails.—The person that hath the nails thus, is of gentle nature, good, and pusillanimous, and a great fear to speak before great persons, or those by whom they are in subjection; as also being guilty of extreme bashfulness.

If about these nails there happens to be an excoriation of the flesh, which is commonly called points—in these large nails it signifies the party given to luxury, yet fearful, but usually given to excess.

When there is at the extremity a white mark, it signifies ruin through negligence. The party has more honesty than subtlety.

White Nails.—He that hath the nails white and long is sickly, and subject to much infirmity by fevers; he is neat, but not very strong, because of his indispositions, much addicted to the company of women, by whom he will be greatly deceived.

Narrow Nails.—The person with such nails is desirous of attaining knowledge in the sciences; but if to narrowness they add some degree of length, the person will be led away by ambitious propensities, always aiming at things which he will be unable to obtain.

Round Nails.—These declare a hasty person, yet good-natured and very forgiving; a lover of knowledge, liberal sentiment, doing no one any harm, and acting by his own principles, but too proud of his own abilities.

Long Nails.—When the nails are long, the person is of a good-natured turn, but placing confidence in no man, being from his youth familiar with duplicity, but not practising it, from his strict adherence to virtue.

Fleshy Nails.—This description of nail indicates an idler, loving to sleep, eat, and drink; not delighting in bustle and busy life; one who prefers a narrow income without industry, to one of opulence to be acquired by activity and diligence.

Little Nails.—Little round nails discover a person to be obstinately angry, seldom pleased, inclining to hate every one, as conceiving himself superior to others, though without any reasons, and, ta.

circle, and face up۰ ۰ ۰ d Nails.—A melancholy person, one who through choice leads a sedentary life, and would willingly give up all things for the sake of study, and to improve in the learned and metaphysical branches of philosophy.

Red and Spotted Nails.—Choleric and martial, delighting in cruelty and war; his chief pleasure being in plundering towns, where every ferocious particle in human nature is glutted to satiety.

When you find any black spots upon the nails, they always signify evil, as white ones are a token of good.

SIGNS OR INSTANCES OF GOOD AND ILL FORTUNE ON PARTICULAR DAYS.

Antipater Sidonius, the poet, throughout the whole space of his life, every year, for one day only, that is, the day whereon he was born, was seized with a fever; and when he had lived to a great age, by the certain return of his wonted disease, he died upon his birth day.

The Emperor Charles V. was born on the day of Matthias, the apostle, on which day also, in the course of his life, was King Francis taken by him in battle, and the victory likewise won at Biccoque; he was also elected and crowned emperor on the same day, and many other great fortunes befel him still on that day.

M. Ofilius Hilarius, an actor of comedies, after he had pleased the people upon his birthday, kept a feast in his own house, and when supper was set forth upon the table, he called for a mess of hot broth to sup off; and withal casting his eye upon the visor he had worn that day in the play, he fitted it again to his face, and taking off the garland, which he wore upon his bare head, he set it thereupon; in this posture, disguised as he sat, he was stark dead, and cold, too, before any person in the company perceived any such thing

King Phillip of Macedon used to celebrate his birthday with extraordinary joy, as the most favorable and fortunate to him of all others. For once upon that day he had a triplicity of good tidings, that he was victor in the chariot race in the Olympic games, that Parmenio, his general, had gained a most important victory and that the Queen of Olympias was delivered of a son, Alexander.

It is worthy to be remembered that Thursday was observed to be a fatal day to King Henry VIII., and to all his posterity for he himself died on Thursday, the 28th of January; King Edward VI., on Thursday, the 9th of July; Queen Mary, on Thursday, the 17th of November, and Queen Elizabeth on Thursday, the 24th of March.

Franciscus Baudenus, an abbot, a citizen of Florence, and well known in the court of Rome, died upon the anniversary of his birthday, which was upon the 12th of December; he was buried in the church of St. Silvester, in Rome, and it was the observation of him that made his funeral elegy, that the number nine did four times happen remarkably in his affairs, he was born on the 19th, and died on the same, being aged twenty-nine, in the year 1579.

Wednesday is said to have been fortunate to Pope Sixtus V., for on that day he was born, on the same day made a monk, on that day created general of his order, on the same day made cardinal, then chosen pope, and finally, on the same day was inaugurated.

STRANGE WAYS THAT MURDER &c. HAVE BEEN DISCOVERED THROUGH DREAMS.

Two friends traveling together in the confines of Arcadia, when they came to Mægara, one took up his lodging in a friend's house, and the other in an inn. He that lodged with his friend, thought he saw in his sleep his fellow-traveler begging his help against the inn-keeper, who was attempting to murder him; upon which he leaped out of bed, with a resolution to see after his friend; but considering further of it, he thought it but a dream, and went to bed again. He was no sooner asleep, but his friend appears a second time wounded and bloody, saying, "Revenge my death, for I am killed by the inn-keeper, and am now carrying towards the gate in a cart covered with dung." The man still fancied it was a melancholy dream; and yet thinking it would be an unpardonable neglect if there should be any truth in it, made haste to the gate, and there finding a cart loaded with dung, as the apparition had told him, forced the cart to be unladen, and to his sorrow found the corpse of his murdered friend, for which the inn-keeper was prosecuted and hanged.

"Whilst I lived at Prague," saith an English gentleman, "and one night had sat up very late drinking at a feast, early in the morning the sunbeams glancing on my face as I lay in my bed, I dreamed that a shadow passing by told me that my father was dead. At which, awaking all in a sweat, and affected with this dream, I rose and wrote the day and hour, and all circumstances thereof, in a paper book, which book, with many other things, I put into a barrel, and sent it from Prague to Stode, thence to be conveyed into England. And now being at Noremberg, a merchant of a noble family well acquainted with me and my relations, arrived there, who told me that my father died some months past. When I returned into England four years after, I would not open the barrel I sent from Prague, nor look into the paper book in which I had writen this dream, till I had called my sisters and some other friends to be witnesses; where myself and they were astonished to see my written dream answer the very day of my father's death.

A citizen of Milan was asked for a debt as owing by his dead father; and when he was in some trouble about it, the image of his dead father appeared to him in his sleep, told him the whole process of the business, "that the debt was by him paid in his life time, and that if he looked in such a place, he should find a writing under the hand of his creditor, wherein he did acknowledge himself satisfied." Directly he awoke from his sleep, and reflecting upon his dream, he searched and found all things agreeable to what he had dreamed. St. Austin saith, that this very writing was seen by him.

Upon a sally being made upon some of the forces of Alexander the Great, out of Harmata, a city of the Brachmans, many of his soldiers were wounded with poisoned darts, and as well as those that were lightly, as those that were deeper wounded, daily perished. Amongst the wounded was Ptolomy, a great captain, and exceedingly dear to Alexander; when, therefore, in the night he had been solicitous about his welfare, as one whom he tenderly loved, he seemed in his sleep to see a dragon holding a certain medicinal herb in his mouth, and withal informing him both of the virtue it had, and of the place where it grew. He arose, found the herb, bruised it, and applied it to Ptolomy's wound; and by this means that great ancestor of the royal family in Egypt was speedily restored.

THE PERFECT FORTUNE TELLER.

A rich vessel of gold being stolen out of the Temple of Hercules, Sophocles (by a Genius) was showed the resemblance and name of the thief in his sleep, which for the first and second time, he neglected; but being troubled a third night, he went to the Areopagi, to whom he made relation of what had passed. They, upon no other evidence, summoned the party before them, who, after strict examination confessed the fact, and made restitution of the vessel. For which discovery the Temple was ever after called *Templum Hercules Indicis.* "The Temple of Hercules the Discoverer."

Alexander, the philosopher, (a man known to be free from superstition) reports of himself, "that sleeping one night he saw his mother's funeral soleminized, being then a day's journey from thence. Whereupon he, waking in great sorrow and many tears, told the dream to divers of his acquaintance and friends. The time being punctually observed, certain word was brought him the next day after, that at the same hour as his dream was his mother expired.

Thomas Wotton, a little before his death, dreamed that the University Treasury was robbed by townsmen and poor scholars, and that the number was five; and being that day to write to his son Henry, at Oxford, he thought it was worth so much pains, as by a postscript in his letter to make a slight inquiry of it. The letter which was written in Kent, came to his son the very morning after the night in which the robbery was committed, and when the City and University were both in a perplexed inquest after the thieves, then did Sir Henry Wotton show his father's letter, and by it such light was given of this work of darkness, that the five persons were presently discovered and apprehended. Without putting the University to so much as the casting of a figure.

FOREBODING DREAMS.

There are some queer statements on record connected with foreboding dreams. Lord Littleton, it is said, was warned of his death by a dream. Brandt in his "Popular Antiquitirs," tells of a seaman who suffered much from superstitious fears. When on the night-watch, he would see sights and hear noises — in the rigging and the deep—which kept him in a perpetual fever of alarm. One day the poor fellow imagined the Evil One visited him, and told him he had only three days to live.

THE PERFECT FORTUNE TELLER.

His messmates all laughed at him. The next day he told them the arch fiend had paid him a second visit, announcing a repetition of the melancholy tidings. His friends expostulated with him, but it was no use. Now, the morning of the fatal day happened to be stormy, and the dreamer, with others, was sent aloft. Before he ascended he bade his messmates farewell, telling them he had received a third warning, and he was confident he should be dead before night. He ascended into the rigging with this terrible foreboding on his mind, and, losing his hold, fell upon the deck and was killed. Now, we can account for the result here, by supposing the sailor to have taken too much strong drink before leaving port, and when at sea, and deprived of liquor, to have been afflicted with delirium tremens so terrible that the dreams and their results were quite natural. Probably the causes of all these forewarnings can be traced as easily; in other words, they lie in a weak or disordered mind and a shattered system. Take the case of Galba, the successor of Nero. It is said his death was foretold him by a marble statue of Fortune, which stood in the Tusculum, at Rome. It seems he had coquetted with this statue, as well as another—the capotoline Venus—and that he had, in the excess of his admiration, adorned Fortune with a splendid necklace of brilliants. The charms of Venus, however, finally prevailed over those of Fortune, and the necklace was ultimately presented to the Goddess of Beauty. In consequence of this, the slighted, insulted Fortune, appeared to Galba in his sleep, and, upbraiding him with his infidelity, told him he should be deprived of all the gifts she had lavished upon him, soon after which he died. Now Galba was seventy-two years old when he was slain by his soldiers, and what with rage and a fruition of honors, was reduced to a very weak state of mind, or he never would have, just before that event, gone into ecstacies about the marble statue. It may be inferred, hence, that the very imbecility, or second childishness, which would prompt him to hang a necklace of diamonds around the neck of a marble form, would not be able to overcome its indignant visitation in a dream, because of bestowing its property on a rival. Again, he saw his fate in his own wickedness and folly. He knew that the outraged Roman soldiers would soon vent their hatred in his death.

THE PERFECT FORTUNE TELLER.

TO KNOW THE TEMPER AND DISPOSITION OF EVERY ONE.

THE SIGNS OF A CHOLERIC DISPOSITION ARE:

1.—The habit of the body hot in touch, dry, lean, hard, and hairy.

2.—The color of the face yellow.

3.—A natural dryness of the mouth and tongue.

4 —The thirst great and frequent.

5.—Activity and inquietude of the body

6.—The pulse hard, swift, and often beating.

7.—The spittle bitter.

8.—The dreams are most of yellow things, of brawls, of fights, and quarrels.

THE SIGNS OF A SANGUINE CONSTITUTION ARE:

1.—The habit of the body hot in touch, fleshy, soft and hairy.

2.—The color of the body fresh, sanguine and lively.

3.—A natural and constant blush in the face.

4.—The pulse soft, moist and full.

5.—The spittle sweet.

6.—Dreams most commonly of red things, of beauty, feasting, dancing, music, and all jovial and pleasing recreations.

7.—A continual habit of pleasantness and affability.

8 —Often affected with jests, mirth and laughter.

THE SIGNS OF A PHLEGMATIC CONSTITUTION ARE:

1.—The habit of the body cold and moist; in touch, soft, fat, gross, and not hairy.

2.—A constant natural whiteness or wanness in the face.

3.—The pulse soft, slow and rare.

4.—The thirst little and seldom desiring drink.

5.—The dreams usually are of white things, floods, inundaions, and accidents belonging to water.

6.—Sleep much and frequent.

7.—Slowness and dullness of the body to exercise.

THE SIGNS OF A MELANCHOLY CONSTITUTION ARE:

1.—The body in touch, cold, dry, lean and smooth.

2.—The body of a dark, dull, gloomy, leaden color.

3.—The spittle in small quantities and sour.

4.—Pulse little, rare and hard.

5.—They dream of terrible things, as ghosts, wild beasts, etc.

6.—Greatly oppressed with fear.

7.—Constancy in the performance of the thing intended.

THE SIGNS OF A GENEROUS PERSON ARE:

1.—The forehead large, fleshy, plain and smooth.

2.—The eye moist and shining.

3.—The countenance expressing joy and content.

4.—The voice pleasant.

5.—The motion of the body slow, etc.

THE SIGNS OF AN ILL-NATURED PERSON ARE

1.—The form of the body meager and lean.

2.—The forehead cloudy, sullen and wrinkled.

3.—The eye cast down and malicious.

4.—A nimble tongue.

5.—Walking a short, quick, uneven pace.

6.—A secret murmuring to himself as he walks.

PHYSIOGNOMY.

A knowledge of this science furnishes us the infallible means of discovering the temper and the mind by the countenance or face. Like its kindred sciences, Phrenology and Chiromancy, it must be carefully studied, and considerable practice is necessary to enable us to use it with absolute correctness. In determining characters we should never depend upon a single feature to the exclusion of the rest, for an evil tendency of the mind, as indicated by a portion of the countenance, may be entirely overbalanced and counteracted by characteristics as indicated by some better favored feature.

THE FACE IN GENERAL.

1. The face that is round, plump and ruddy tells the person to be of an agreeable temper, faithful in love; in a man, it denotes him to be easily led astray.

2. The face that is smooth, well-proportioned features, denotes a good disposition, but inclined to be suspicious; strongly addicted to the pleasures of love, and agreeable conversation.

3. A face with very prominent cheek bones and thin, shows a very restless disposition, fretful, and always imagining evil.

4. A person naturally pale denotes the person amorous.

5. A face of a sickly white denotes a very malicious disposition, false and very inconstant.

6. A countenance that is pleasant, with red hair, shows the party to be very talkative, and at times very quarrelsome, positive in their own opinions, and very amorous.

7. The person whose features are strong, coarse and unpleasant to the eye, is of a selfish, brutal, rough and unsociable disposition; greedy of money, harsh in expressions, but will sometimes fawn with a bad grace to gain his ends.

8. A face whose cheek bones jut out with thin jaws is of a restless and thinking disposition, but penetrating and apt to be fretful.

9. A face that is pale by nature, denotes a timorous disposition, but greatly desirous of carnal pleasures.

10. A face that is unequally red, whether streaked or appearing in spots, shows the person to be weak both in mind and body, yielding easily to affliction and sickness.

THE HEAD.

1. The head that is large and round shows that the person has a tolerable understanding, but not near so good as he imagines; however, upon the whole, he is rather harmless, and not so much given to vice.

2. The head that is small and round, or if the face comes tapering, shows the person of an acute, penetrating disposition, much given to bantering and humor, but of very great sensibility.

3. The head that is flat on either side, and deep from the face to the back, shows the person to be of a good understanding, deep penetration, great memory, and of an even and agreeable temper, but of slow belief, and not easily imposed upon.

THE FOREHEAD.

1. The forehead flat in the middle, shows either sex to be proud and ungenerous, very curious to know the secrets of others, and very violent in love affairs.

2. If the forehead projects over the eye brows, running flat up

to the hair, the possessor will be insolent and treacherous, injuring every one, but never forgiving an injury

3. The forehead that is large, round and smooth announces the lady or gentlemen to be frank, open, generous, free and good-natured, and a safe companion; of a good understanding, scorning to be guilty of any mean action; faithful to his promises, just in his dealings, steadfast in his engagements, and sincere in his affections; he will enjoy a moderate state of health.

4. If there be a hollow across the forehead, in the middle, with a ridge as of flesh above, and another below, the gentleman will be a good scholar, and the lady a great manufacturer, or attentive to whatever occupation she may be engaged in. They will be warm in argument or debate—they will be firm and steady in any point they fix their minds upon, and by their perseverance will generally carry their object, yet they will meet with many crosses, but will bear them with patience.

5. If the temples are hollow, with the bones advancing towards the forehead on either side, so that the space between must be necessarily flat, with a small channel or indenture rising from the upper part of the nose to the hair, the gentleman or lady will be of a daring and intrepid temper, introducing themselves into matters where they have no business, desirous of passing for wits, and of a subtle and enterprising nature; greedy of praise, quick in quarrel, and of a wandering disposition; very lewd, and full of resentment when they feel their pride hurt. In short, they delight in mischief making and quarrels.

THE EYES.

1. The eyes that are large, full and clear, denotes the possessor to be void of deceit, of an agreeable disposition, modest and bashful, particularly in affairs of love.

2. The eye that is small but advanced in the head shows the gentleman or lady to be of quick wit, sound constitution, lively genius, agreeable company and conversation, good morals, but rather inclined to jealousy; attentive to business, fond of frequently changing his place, punctual in fulfilling his engage

...ents, warm in love, prosperous in his undertakings, and generally fortunate in most things.

3. The gentleman or lady whose eyes are sunk in the head, is of a jealous, distrustful, malicious, and envious nature; deceitful in their words and actions, never to be depended upon; cunning in overreaching others, vain-glorious, and associates with lewd or bad company.

4. The gentleman or lady who squints, or have their eyes turned awry, will be of a penurious disposition, but punctual in their dealings.

5. A black eye is lively, brisk, and penetrating, and proves the person who possesses it to be of sprightly wit, lively conversation, not easily imposed upon, of a sound understanding, but if taken on the weak side, may be led astray for a while.

6. A hazel eye shows the person to be of a subtle, piercing and frolicsome turn, rather inclined to be arch, and sometimes mischievous, but good-natured at the bottom. He will be strongly inclined to love, and not over delicate in the means of gratifying that propensity.

7. A blue eye shows the person to be of a meek and gentle temper, affable and good-natured, credulous, and incapable of violent attachments; ever modest, cool, and undisturbed by turbulent passions, of a strong memory, in constitution neither robust nor delicate, subject to no violent impressions from the vicissitudes of life, whether good or bad.

8. A gray eye denotes the person to be of weak intellect, devoid of wit, but a plain, plodding, downright drudge, that will act as he is spirited up by others. He will be slow in learning anything that requires attention; he, however, will be just to the best of his understanding.

9. A wall eye denotes the person to be of a hasty, passionate, and ungovernable temper, subject to sudden and violent anger; haughty to his equals and superiors, but mild and affable to his inferiors.

10. A red, or as it is vulgarly called, a saucer eye, denotes the person to be selfish, deceitful, and proud, and furious in anger, fertile in the invention of plots, and indefatigible in his resolutions to bring them to bear.

11. A person of downcast eyes, when speaking to you, is an enemy, a deceiver, and a designing person. This fault is very bad in a person of very small face and features, a low forehead, and broad chin turning rather upward; for you may expect to find evil in them; carefully avoid a person that does not look you in the face when you are speaking to them.

THE NOSE.

1. A great nose shows a good man; a little nose a deceitful person. A sharp nose denotes an angry person and a scold; thick and low, a person of bad manners.

2. A nose that comes even on the ridge, flat on the sides, with little or no hollow between the eyes, declares the man to be sulky, indolent, disdainful, treacherous, and self-sufficient; if it has a point descending over the nostrils, he is avaricious and unfeeling, vain-glorious and ignorant; peevish, jealous, quick in resentment, yet a coward at the bottom.

3. A nose that rises with a sudden bulge a little below the eyes, and then falls again into a kind of hollow below, is petulent and noisy, void of science, and of a very light understanding.

4. The nose that is small, slender and peaked, shows the person to be of a fearful disposition, jealous, fretful and insidious, ever suspicious of those about him, catching at every word that he can interpret to his own advantage to ground his dispute upon, and also very curious to know what is said and done.

5. The nose that is small, tapering, round in the nostrils, and cocked up, shows the person to be ingenious, smart, and of a quick apprehension, giddy, and seldom looking into consequences; but generous; agreeable, so as to carefully avoid giving offence; but resolute in doing himself justice when he receives an injury.

THE LIPS.

1. The lips that are thick, soft and long, announces the person to be of weak intellect credulous, and slightly peevish; but by a little soothing easily brought back to a good humor. He is much addicted to the pleasures of love, and scarcely moderate in the enjoyment of them; yet he is upright in his conduct, and of a timorous temper.

2. If the under lip is much thicker than the upper, and more prominent, the person is of a weak understanding, but artful, knavish, and given to chicanery to the full extent of his ability.

3. The lips that are moderately plump and even, declare the person to be good-humored, humane, sensible, judicious and just, neither giddy nor torpid, but pursuing in every particular a just medium.

4. The lips that are thin and sunk inwards, denotes the person to be of a subtle and persevering disposition, everlasting in hatred, and never sparing any pains to compass his revenge; in love or friendship much more moderate and uncertain.

5. Thin lips with a little mouth, show an effeminate person; slender, thin and fine lips betoken eloquence; fleshy and great lips, a fool. And those whose teeth project are generally unfaithful; also much addicted to the love of strange women.

THE CHIN.

1. The chin that is round, with a hollow between it and the lip, shows the person to be of a good-humored disposition, kind and honest; he is sincere in his friendship, and ardent in his love; his understanding is good, and his genius capacious. If he has a dimple, it makes him better.

2. The chin that comes down flat from the edge of the lip, and ends in a kind of chisel form, shows the person to be silly, credulous, ill-tempered, and greedy of unmerited honors; captious, wavering, and unsteady; he will affect great modesty in the presence of others, though he will not scruple to do the vilest actions when he thinks himself secure from discovery.

3. The chin that is pointed upwards, shows the person to be much given to contrivances. However fair he may speak to you, you can never depend on **his** friendship, as his purpose is only to make you subservient to his own designs. In love his generosity will be of the same stamp.

4. A long chin, especially in a married female, denotes her to be of a wicked disposition, and in a man, very indiscreet and talkative ; a little chin shows inveteracy and malice ; a broad chin poking forward denotes the possessor to be deceitful and ungrateful, and capable of imposing on their best friends, and of a debauched life.

5. A round chin and dimpled shows good nature, but much addicted to pleasure ; those who have a valley at the joining of the jaws are capable of treachery. If the forehead is well formed and smooth it is a sign that the possessor is generous, tender, and good-natured, possessing a good share of understanding, faithful in business, and sincere in his affections ; but if this is accompanied by a long face, is greatly given to debauchery, and though at times fond of his partner and near connections, yet he is very inconstant.

THE HAIR.

1. The gentleman whose hair is very black and smooth, hanging far over his shoulders, and in large quantity, is mild but resolute; cool, until greatly provoked; not much inclined to excess of any kind, but he may be persuaded to it. He is constant in his attachments, and not liable to m ny misfortunes.

2. A lady of the same kind of hair is moderate in her desires of every kind, addicted to reflection, and though not subject to violence in love, is steady in her attachments, and no enemy to its pleasures; of a constitution neither vigorous nor feeble.

3. If the hair is very black, short and curling, the gentleman will be much given to liquor, somewhat quarrelsome, and of an unsettled temper; more amorous, and less steady in his undertakings, but ardent at the beginning of an enterprise. He will be desirous of riches, but will often be disappointed in his wishes therein.

The same may be said of a lady.

5. A gentleman with dark brown, long and smooth hair is generally of a robust constitution; obstinate in his temper, eager in his pursuits, a lover of the fair sex, fond of variety, in his ordinary pursuits exceedingly curious, and of a flexible disposition. He will live long, unless guilty of early intemperance.

6. A lady of the same kind of hair will be nearly the same as the gentleman, but more steady in her conduct and attachments, especially in love. She will be of a good constitution, have many children, enjoy good health and a reasonable share of happiness.

7. If the hair is short and bushy it will make very little alteration in the gentleman or lady, but that the gentleman will be more forward to strike when provoked, and the lady will be more of a scold.

8. A gentleman with light brown, long, smooth hair, is of a peaceable, even and rather generous temper; will prevent mischief if in his power, but when very much provoked will strike furiously; but is afterwards sorry for his passion, and soon appeased; strongly attached to the company of ladies, and will protect them from insult. Upon the whole, he is in general an amicable character, affable and kind.

9. A lady with the same kind of hair is tender-hearted, but hasty in temper; neither obstinate nor haughty; her inclinations to love never unreasonable; her constitution will be good, but she will be seldom very fortunate.

10. A gentleman with fair hair will be of a weak constitution; his mind given much to reflection, especially in religious matters. He will be assiduous in his occupation, but not given to rambling; very moderate in his amorous wishes, but will not live to an old age.

11. A lady of this colored hair is of a good constitution; never to be diverted from her purposes; passionate in love affairs; never easy unless in company, and delights in hearing herself praised, especially for beauty; delights in dancing and strong exercises, and commonly lives to a great age.

12. A gentleman with long hair is cunning, artful and deceitful; he is much addicted to traffic of some kind, restless in his disposition, constantly roving, and desirous of enjoying the pleasures of love. He is covetous of getting money, and

spends it foolishly; he is indefatigible, and no obstacle will induce him to forsake his enterprise until he has seen the issue of it. He is inclined to timidity, but by reflection may correct it, and pass for a man of courage.

13. A lady of the same kind of hair is glib of tongue, talkative and vain; her temper is impatient and fiery, and will not submit to contradiction; she has a constant flow of spirits, and much given to the pleasures of love. However delicate her spirits may seem, her constitution is generally vigorous; but she seldom lives to see old age, for obvious reasons; her promises are seldom to be depended on, because the next object that engrosses her attention makes her forgetful of everything that preceded it, and will always resent any disappointment she may meet with.

14. If the hair falls off at the fore part of the head, the person will be easily led, though otherwise rational, and will often be duped when he thinks he is acting right; he will likewise frequently meet with disappointments in money matters, which will either hurt his credit, or force him to shorten his expenses.

15. If the hair falls off behind, he will be obstinate, peevish, passionate and fond of commanding others, though he has no right, and will grow angry if his advice is not followed. However preposterous, he will be fond of hearing and telling old stories and tales of ghosts and fairies, but will be a good domestic man, and provide for his family to the utmost of his power.

16. If the hair forms an arch round the forehead, without being much indented at the temples, both the gentleman and the lady will be innocent, credulous, moderate in all their desires, and though not ardent in their pursuits, will still be persevering. They will be modest, good-natured, prosperous and happy.

17. If the hair is indented at the temples, the person will be affable, steady, good-natured, prudent, and attentive to business, of a solid constitution, and long lived.

18. If the hair descends low upon the forehead, the person will be selfish and designing; of a surly disposition, unsociable, and given to drinking. He will also be addicted to avarice, and his mind will always be intent upon the means of carrying on his schemes.

THE PERFECT FORTUNE TELLER.

THE EYEBROWS.

1. When the eyebrows meet across the nose, and are large, the person is uncommonly harsh, ungenerous, unsettled and designing, though very proud.

2. If the eyebrows are very hairy, and that hair long and curled, with several of the hairs starting out, the gentleman or lady is of a gloomy disposition, litigous and quarrelsome, although a coward; greedy after the affairs of this world, perpetually brooding over some melancholy subject and not an agreeable companion. He will be diffident, penurious, and weak in his understanding; never addicted to any kind of learning. He will pretend much friendship, but will make his affected passion subservient to his pecuniary designs, and also given to drinking.

3. If a gentleman or lady has long eyebrows, with some long hairs, they will be of a fickle disposition, weak-minded, credulous and vain, always seeking after novelties, and neglecting their own business; they will be talkative, pert and disagreeable in company; very fond of contradiction, but will not bear disappointment patiently; and also will be much addicted to drinking.

4. If the eyebrows are thick and even, that is, without any or with few starting hairs, the gentleman or lady will be of an agreeable temper, sound understanding, and tolerable wit; moderately addicted to pleasure, fearful of giving offense, but intrepid and persevering in support of right; charitable and generous, sincere in their professions of love and friendship, and enjoy a good constitution.

5. If the eyebrow is small, thin of hair, and even, the gentleman or lady will be weak-minded, timorous, superficial, and not to be depended on; they will be desirous of knowledge, but will not have patience and assiduity enough to give it the necessary attention; they will be desirous of praise for worthy actions, but will not have the spirit or perseverance enough to perform them in that degree of excellence that is requisite to attract the notice of wise men. They will be of a delicate constitution.

6. If the eyebrow is thick of hair towards the nose, and goes off suddenly very thin, ending in a point, the gentleman or lady will be surly, capricious, jealous, fretful, and easily provoked to rage; in their love they will be intemperate.

THE NOSTRILS.

The nostrils thick and strong, betoken strength; if round, fair, drawn in length, merry and courageous. The nostrils narrow and round betoken a foolish person.

THE MOUTH.

A large mouth, with upper lip hanging over, signifies a foolish unsteadfast person.

THE BODY.

Strength of Body is known by stiff hair, large bones, firm and robust limbs, short muscular neck, firm and erect, the head broad and high, the forehead short, hard and peaked, with bristly hair, large feet, rather thick and broad, a harsh, unequal voice, and choleric complexion.

Weakness of Body is distinguished by a small ill-proportioned head, narrow shoulders, soft skin, and melancholy complexion.

The Signs of Long Life are strong teeth, a sanguine temperament, middle size, large, deep, and ruddy lines in the hand; large muscles, stooping shoulders, full chest, firm flesh, clear complexion, slow growth, wide ears and large eyelids.

Short Life may be inferred from a thick tongue, the appearance of grinders before the age of puberty, thin, straggling and uneven teeth, confused lines in the hand, of a quick but small growth.

A Good Genius may be expected from a thin skin, middle stature, blue bright eyes, fair complexion, straight and pretty strong hair, and affable aspect, the eyebrows joined, moderation in mirth, an open, cheerful countenance, and the temples a little concave.

A Dunce may be known by a swollen neck, plump arms, sides and loins, a round head, concave behind, a large fleshy forehead, pale eyes, a heavy dull look, small joints, snuffling nostrils, and a proneness to laughter, little hands, and ill-proportioned head, either too big or too little, blubber lips, short fingers, and thick legs.

Fortitude is promised from a wide mouth, a sonorous voice, grave, slow, and always equal, upright posture, large eyes, pretty open and steadfast, the hair high above the forehead, the head much compressed or flattened, the forehead square and high, the extremities large and robust, the neck firm though not fleshy, a large, corpulent chest, and brown complexion.

Boldness is characterized by a prominent mouth, rugged appearance, rough forehead, arched eyebrows, large nostrils and teeth, short neck, great arms, ample chest, square shoulders, and a forward countenance.

Prudence is generally distinguished by a head which is flat on the sides, broad square forehead a little concave in the middle, a soft voice, a large chest, thin hair, light eyes, either blue, brown or black, large ears, and an aquiline nose.

A Good Memory is commonly attached to those who are smaller, yet better formed in the upper than in the lower parts, not fat but fleshy, of a fair delecate skin, with the poll of the head uncovered, crooked nose, teeth thick set, large ears, with plenty of cartilage.

A Bad Memory is observable in persons who are larger in their superior than inferior parts, fleshy though dry and bald.

A Good Imagination and Thoughtful Disposition is distinguished by a large prominent forehead, a fixed and attentive look, slow respiration, and an inclination of the head.

A Good Sight is enjoyed by those persons who have generally black, thick, straight eye-lashes, large bushy eyebrows, concave eyes, contracted as it were inwards.

Short-Sighted People have a stern, earnest look, small, short eyebrows, large pupils, and prominent eyes.

Sense of Hearing. Those who possess the same in perfection, have ears well furnished with gristle, well channeled and hairy.

The Sense of Smelling is most perfect in those who have large noses, descending very near the mouth, neither too moist nor too dry.

THE PERFECT FORTUNE TELLER.

A Nice Faculty of Tasting is peculiar to such as have a spongy, porous, soft tongue, well moistened with saliva, yet not wet.

Delicacy in the Touch belongs to those who have a soft skin, sensible nerves, and nervous sinews, moderately warm and dry.

Irascibility is accompanied by an erect posture, a clear skin, a solemn voice, open nostrils, moist temples, displaying superficial veins, thick neck, equal use of both hands quick pace, blood-shot eyes, large, unequal, ill-arranged teeth, and choleric disposition.

Timorousness resides where we find a concave neck, pale color, weak winking eyes, soft eyes, soft hair, smooth plump breast, shrill, tremulous voice, small mouth, thin lips, broad thin hands, and small, shambling foot.

Melancholy is denoted by a wrinkled countenance, dejected eyes, meeting eyebrows, slow pace, fixed look, and deliberate respiration.

An amorous Disposition may be known by a fair, slender face, a redundancy of hair, rough temples, broad forehead, moist shining eyes, wide nostrils, narrow shoulders, hairy hands and arms, well shaped legs.

Gaiety attends a serene, open forehead, rosy, agreeable countenance, a sweet musical tone of voice, an agile body, and soft flesh.

Envy appears with a wrinkled forehead, frowning, dejected, and squinting look, a pale, melancholy countenance, and a dry, rough skin.

Intrepidity often resides in a small body, with red curled hair, ruddy countenance, frowning eyebrows, arched and meeting, eyes blue or yellowish, large mouth, and red lines in the hand.

Gentleness or compalcency may be distinguished by a soft and moist palm, frequency of shutting the eyes, soft movement, slow speech, soft, straight and lightish colored hair.

Bashfulness may be discovered by moist eyes, never wide open, eyebrows frequently lowered, blushing cheeks, moderate pace, slow and submissive speech, bent body, and glowing ears of a purple hue.

THE PERFECT FORTUNE TELLER.

Temperance or sobriety is accompanied with equal respiration, a moderated sized mouth, smooth temples, eyes of an ordinary size; either fair on azure, and a short, flat body.

Strength of mind is signified by light curled hair, a small body, shining eyes, but a little depressed, a grave, intense voice, bushy beard, large, broad back and shoulders.

Pride stands confessed with large eyebrows, a large prominent mouth, a broad chest, slow pace, erected head, shrugging shoulders, and staring eyes.

Luxury dwells with a ruddy or pale complexion, downy temples, bald pate, little eyes, thick neck, corpulent body, large nose, thin eyebrows, and hands covered with a kind of down.

Loquacity may be expected from a bushy beard, broad fingers, pointed tongue, eyes of a ruddy hue, a large prominent upper lip, and sharp pointed nose.

Perverseness may be dreaded when we perceive a high forehead, firm, short, thick, immovable neck, quick speech, immoderate laughter, fiery eyes, **and short fleshy hands and fingers**

SIGNS AND AUGURIES.

However skeptical some persons may profess to be on the subject of signs, auguries, and forewarnings, still few will venture to deny that in innumerable instances those admonitions and forewarnings have been speeddily followed by events of a pleasant or a painful nature to those who have received them. The belief in signs and augurics has been cherished by mankind ever since the creation ; and this remarkable faculty is not confined to the human family alone, but lower animals possess it, some of them in extraordinary degree. The following are a few of the multifarious signs and auguries which admonish and forewarn mankind at one time or another.

Should you be the subject of a deep depression of spirits, contrary to your usual constitutional buoyancy and liveliness, it is a sign that you are about to receive some agreeable intelligence.

If the crown of your head itches more than ordinary, you may expect to be advanced to a more honorable position in life.

Should the hair on your head come off when combing in greater quatities than usual, it is a sign that you will soon be the subject of a severe attack of illness.

If your right eyebrow should immoderately itch, be assured you are going to look upon a pleasant sight—a long-absent friend, or a long-estranged but now reconciled lover.

Should your left eye-brow be visited with a tantalizing itching, it is a sign that you will look upon a painful sight—the corpse of a valued friend or your lover walking with a favored rival.

A ringing in your ear is an augury that you will shortly hear some pleasant news.

THE PERFECT FORTUNE TELLER.

A ringing in your left ear is a sign that you will in a short time receive intelligence of a very unpleasant nature.

When your left ear tingles, some one is back-biting you.

A violent itching of the nose foretells trouble and sorrow to those who experience it.

An itching of the lips is a sign that some one is speaking disrespectfully of you.

When you are affected by an itching on the back of your neck, be assured that either yourself or some one nearly related to you, is about to suffer a violent death.

An itching on the right shoulder, signifies that you will shortly receive a gift.

When you feel an itching sensation on your left shoulder, be sure that you are about to bear a heavy burden of sorrow and trouble.

If your right elbow joint itches, you may expect shortly to hear some intelligence that will give you extreme pleasure.

Should you be annoyed with a violent itching on your left elbow joint, you may be sure that some vexatious disapointment will be experienced by you.

If you feel an itching on the palm of your right hand, you may expect soon to receive some money which you have been long expecting.

When the palm of your left hand itches, you may expect to be called upon to pay some money for a debt which you have not personally incurred,

An itching on the spine of your back is a sign that you will shortly be called upon to bear a heavy burden of sorrow and trouble.

An itching on your loins is an indication that you will soon recieve an addition to your family, if married; if single, that you are on the eve of marriage.

When you are affected with an itching on the belly, expect to be invited to a feast upon choice collection of savory meats.

When either or both of your thighs itch, be assured that you are about to change your sleeping apartment.

If you have an itching sensation in your right knee, depend upon it that you will shortly undergo a remarkable and beneficial change in your previous course of life, and become religiously inclined.

If a similar sensation prevails in your left knee, you may expect to undergo a change in your deportment of an unfavorable nature.

An itching sensation on the shins, foretells that you will be visited with a painful and long-continued affliction.

When your ankle-joints itch, be sure that you are about to be united to one whom you love, if single; if married, that your domestic comforts will be largely increased.

When the sole of your right foot itches, you may be assured that you are about to undertake a journey from which you will derive much pleasure and enjoyment.

Should you experience a similar sensation on the sole of your left foot, you may expect to be called upon to take a journey of an unpleasant and melancholy nature.

THE WEATHER.

In the evening, when the horizon in the west is tinged with a ruddy glow, it is a sign that bright and dry weather will speedily follow.

When the sky appears ruddy in the east in the evening, changeable weather may be confidently anticipated.

Should the horizon in the north wear a ruddy appearance in the evening, stormy and boisterous weather may be expected.

If the clouds in the south are ruddy in the evening, sunshiny and rainy weather will prevail for some time afterward.

When the face of the moon is partially obscured by a light thin vapor, rain will shortly follow.

THE PERFECT FORTUNE TELLER.

When the rays of the sun at mid-day are more than ordinarily dazzling, rainy weather will shortly succeed.

In summer time when the swallows fly near to the ground, rainy weather will assuredly soon follow.

The shrill crowing of the cock during rainy weather is a sign that drought will speedily prevail.

When the smoke from the chimney falls down toward the ground, instead of rising upward, it is a sign that rainy weather will soon follow.

If on a foggy morning in summer the fog rises upward, it will be a fine day; if the fog falls to the ground, it will be wet.

When, in summer time, you see cattle grazing in a field and gathering together in groups, be assured that a thunder-storm is approaching.

When you see the fowls in the farm-yard flocking together under some covert, be assured that ungenial weather is about to succeed.

When the crows on flying over your head make an extraordinary and discordant cawing, rain will come on shortly.

When you see your dog or cat more than ordinarily restless, frisking about the house in all directions, be assured that some boisterous weather will shortly follow.

In rainy weather, when you hear the chiriping of the sparrows on the house-top more shrill than usual, it is a sign that clear and dry weather will quickly succeed.

When you see a vapory fluid resting upon a stagnant pond in the fore part of the day, you may conclude that rainy weather will shortly come on. Should the vapor ascend and clear away, a continued draught may be anticipated.

In summer, when the atmosphere is dense and heavy, and there is scarcely a breath of air, be assured that a thunder-storm is coming on.

When the firmament is lighted up with meteoric phenomena, such as falling stars, globes of fire, &c., changeable and boisterous weather may be expected to prevail.

THE PERFECT FORTUNE TELLER.

When the rising sun appears like a solid mass of fervent-heated metal, and no rays appear to emanate therefrom, fine and dry weather may be confidently anticipated.

When the sun sets in a halo of ruddy brightness, genial and bright weather may be fully relied on for the coming day.

When the moon appears of a ruddy hue, stormy and boisterous weather may be expected to follow.

When the stars appear of a sparkling brightness, fine and genial weather may be expected to prevail for some time. Should the stars appear obscure and dim, changeable and rainy weather may be anticipated.

The luminous appearance of the Aurora Borealis, or Northern Lights, in the firmament, fortells the approach of stormy and boisterous weather.

When the setting sun in the autumn or winter seasons appears ruddy, it is a sign that high and boisterous winds may be expected to blow from the north and north-west When the sun at its rising in the autumn or winter seasons appears ruddy, it fortells that high and boisterous winds may be anticipated to blow from the south and south-east.

When the sea-birds are observed flocking toward the shore, storms and tempests may be confidently expected.

When in the early autumn season the migratory birds are seen flocking together, and taking their departure, it is a certain sign that rough and boisterous weather is approaching, and that a severe winter may be anticipated.

When the doves around a dove-cote make a more than ordinary cooing, and frequently pass in and out of their cote, it is a sign that a change of weather is near.

When the robin approaches your habitation, it is a sign that wintery weather will shortly prevail.

When there is a thick vapory mist resting on the tops of high hills in the morning, and remains there during the day, it is a sign that wet and ungenial weather may be anticipated. Should the mist eventually rise upward, and be evaporated by the sun's rays, a return to fine dry weather may be looked for; if, however, the mist falls down into the valley, a continuation of wet weather will prevail.

THE PERFECT FORTUNE TELLER.
TO TELL FORTUNES BY DOMINOES.

Lay them with their faces on the table and shuffle them; hen draw one and see the number, which has its meaning as follows:

Double-six. Receiving a handsome sum of money.

Six-five. Going to a place of public amusement.

Six-four. Law suits and trouble, which can only be avoided by great care.

Six-three. A ride in a carriage.

Six-two. A present of clothing.

Six-one. You will soon perform a friendly action.

Six-blank. Guard against scandal, or you will suffer by your inattention.

Double-five. A new abode to your advantage.

Five-four. A fortunate speculation in business.

Five-three. A visit from a superior.

Five-two. A pleasant excursion on the water.

Five-one. A love intrigue.

Five-blank. A funeral, but not of a relation.

Double-four. Drinking liquor at a distance.

Four-three. A false alarm at your house.

Four-two. Beware of thieves and swindlers. Ladies, take notice of this; it means more than it says.

Four-one. Expect trouble from creditors.

Four-blank. You will receive a letter from an angry friend.

Double-three. A sudden wedding, at which you will be vexed, and by which you will lose a friend.

Three-two. Buy no lottery tickets, nor enter into any game of chance, or you will assuredly lose.

calculations :—If your queen is not amongst them you stay in, your place will be long. If there are three tens in this division you will marry well ; if the ten of spades is next to the seven of diamonds, beware of temptation and seduction.

CHARMS.

CHARM OF THE ROSE.

OR HOW TO TELL WHETHER YOU WILL EVER BECOME RICH.

Take a common full-blown rose, and having thrown flour of sulphur into a chaffing dish of hot coals, hold the rose over the fumes thereof, and if it change to white, you will most assuredly become very rich, but if it change to drab, or nearly white, you will never be very rich, and will meet with great misfortunes.

THE ANNISEED CHARM.

OR HOW TO SUCCEED IN ANY GREAT UNDERTAKING.

If you are going on any great undertaking and wish to succeed in it, you should annoit your head and feet with anniseed, and cross your face and chest with red chalk ; cut three locks of your hair from the back of your head, make a good fire with coke or coal, stand in front of the same, and commit the hair to the flames, repeating the following verse three times without once drawing breath :—

> O sweet anniseed do assist me,
> To succeed in this, and I will bless thee,
> For a great undertaking I want your aid,
> Grant me the same, and my fortune is made.

Watch the fire till the last spark has expired, go to bed at midnight, rise at four, and well cleanse your skin from the annointment, go to bed again until five o'clock, then get up and commence operations, and you will be sure to succeed.

CHARM OF AFFECTION.

OR HOW TO TELL WHETHER YOUR BROTHER OR FATHER, OR ANY OTHER RELATION HAS BEEN SLAIN OR WOUNDED IN A BATTLE THAT HAS JUST BEEN FOUGHT.

When you hear of a battle having been fought, in which your relation has been engaged, take a handful of common salt and place it on a piece of paper, writing paper is best, and place the paper of salt on the middle of a round mahogany table, then get a quarter of an ounce of brimstone, a quarter of an ounce of blue fire and a quarter of an ounce of red, the last three articles you must lay separately on clean white plates, putting them in the form of a triangle round the paper of salt, then take the paper of salt and empty it round the edges of the plates containing the brimstone and the blue and red fire; set them all on fire simultaneously, and if the brimstone burns out first, your relation is safe; if the blue light burns out first, he is wounded; but if the red light burns out first, he has been killed. You must be careful of letting the light touch the salt, or of spilling it upon the table.

CHARM OF THE DOVE.

FOR PROCURING REVELATIONS BY DREAMS.

This must be tried alone, and with profound secresy, between the hours of nine and twelve at night, neither sooner nor later, Take a white dove, and kill it, take out the heart and liver, and roast it till you can powder it on a sheet of white paper, mix one tea-spoonful of this with a drachm of dragon's blood, put them in half a gill of cyprus wine, and drink it on going to bed, previously mix the blood that flows from the bird with wheaten flour, into a cake of the form of a heart, prick it with the first letters of your name, and the form of a Maltese cross; leave the cake baking over the fire, as it will have great influence in your dream.

THE DREAMING CHARM.

FOR DREAMING MORE FULLY ON SUBJECTS PREVIOUSLY DREAMED.

When you dream any particular dream, write it down in a circle, on a round piece of paper, so that the last word comes into the middle, and place it under your pillow on going to bed, and you will dream more fully on the subject.

THE MYSTIC SPELL.

FOR TESTING WHETHER A SUPPOSED FRIEND IS A REAL ONE OR NOT, OR WHETHER YOUR LOVER IS TRUE OR FALSE.

Get three, five, seven, nine, eleven, or thirteen leaden bullets, they must be new, and all of different sizes, and must not have been made by yourself. If you are a male, you must choose even numbers; if a female, odd; we will say, for comparison, that you are a female, well, you get seven bullets, according to the above directions; as the clock strikes ten, you must bury them in the ground, seven inches deep, that is, one inch for every bullet you use, this you must do six consecutive nights, taking them up each day as the clock strikes the same hour, and on the sixth you must sprinkle them with rose-water, or lavender water, (either will do, and any time of the day will do for this), and tie them in your left sock or stocking on going to bed, placing them under your pillow, and if the person you are testing is true, he will appear to you in a vision in the course of the night, if, on the other hand, he is playing you false, you will see nothing.

You must not try this charm or mystic spell with less than *three* or more than *thirteen* bullets, if you do it will destroy the spell, and you might as well let it alone.

THE NEEDLE CHARM, (FOR LOVERS.)

OR HOW TO MAKE AN ANGRY LOVER'S NOSE ITCH UNTIL HE HAS HAD AN INTERVIEW WITH YOU, AND FORGIVEN ANY FAULT THAT HAS OFFENDED HIM.

Get a small piece of red blotting paper, about two inches square and cut a small hole in the center with your scissors, (a knife will not do); take a needle and pierce a small hole in each corner of the paper, then, with another needle, pierce your thumbs and little fingers till the blood flows, then wet two corners of the paper with the blood from your little fingers, and the other two with the blood from your thumbs, let the paper dry and then burn it, repeating the following verse the while:—

> Come to me my lover calm,
> Be generous, kind, and free,
> Come my lover to my arms,
> And I'll ever think of thee.

This done, your lover will have no peace, day or night, until he has seen and forgiven you.

THE CHARM OF LOVE.

OR HOW TO TELL WHETHER YOUR LOVER OR SWEETHEART EVER LOVED ANY ONE ELSE.

Take seven gray peas and one white one, which must have laid in dry salt for three days, and place them round the wick of a tallow candle while it is lighted, and let them stay there for thirty minutes without once snuffing it, then take them out and put them in a small saucepan, let them boil over a slow fire for three hours, but do not look at them the while, then strain them off, and if the gray one has boiled soft and the white one has kept hard, your lover, or sweetheart, never loved any one else, but if the white one boil soft and the gray ones keep hard, he or she has loved some one else.

THE PARCHMENT CHARM.

OR HOW TO MAKE A DYING RELATION THINK OF YOU IN HIS OR HER WILL.

Get a piece of new parchment, and in the right-hand bottom corner write the name of your relative, then write your own underneath, you must then write the sum of money or property that you wish to have left you underneath the two signatures, this done, you hide the parchment in some secret place for three weeks, then you remove it to your clothes box, first soaking the parchment in the blood of a male rabbit, or hare; now the charm or spell is complete, and when your relative dies you will find that what property you have wished for on the parchment has been left you.

CHARM OF THE MYRTLE.

OR HOW TO DREAM OF YOUR INTENDED HUSBAND.

Let any number of young women, not exceeding seven or less than three, assemble in a room, where they are sure to be safe from interlopers, just as the clock strikes eleven at night, take from your bosom a sprig of myrtle, which you must have worn there all day, and fold it up in a bit of tissue paper, then light up a small chafing dish of charcoal, and on it each maiden throw nine hairs from her head, and a pareing of her toe and finger nails, then let each sprinkle a small quantity of myrtle and frankincense in the charcoal, and while the odoriferous vapor rises, fumigate your myrtle (this plant or tree is consecrated to Venus) with it. Go to bed while the clock is striking twelve, place the myrtle exactly under your head, and you will be sure to dream of your future husband. Observe, it is no manner of use trying this charm if you are not a real virgin, and the myrtle hour of performance must be past in strict silence.

THE BEAN, PEA, AND OAT CHARM.

TO TELL WHETHER YOUR FUTURE HUSBAND IS A DRUNKARD, OR IN THE HABIT OF STOPPING OUT LATE AT NIGHT.

Get seven beans, any sort will do, and seven gray peas, and seven black oats, set them in three different flower-pots, at the hour of three in the morning, no other time will do, water them with cold spring water every night as the clock is striking twelve for three consecutive nights, and on the fourth night look at them, by removing the mould, and if the beans and peas and oats have all began to shoot, your future husband will neither be a drunkard, or stop out late at night, but if none of have begun to shoot it will be the reverse.

CHARM OF THE CANDLES,

OR HOW TO TELL WHETHER A CHILD BELONGING TO YOU OR ANY OTHER PERSON SHALL LIVE OR DIE.

Get three penny mould candles, and with a pin write the christian name of the father on one of the candles, and the name of the mother on another, and the name of the child upon the third, then set all three burning, and if the candle with the child's name written upon it burns out first, the child will not live, if the one with the mother's name written upon it burns out first, the child will be married early, but if the one with the father's name written upon it burns out first, the child will never be married, but will live to a great age.

THE FIGURE CHARM.

OR HOW TO KNOW IF A CHILD NEW BORN SHALL LIVE OR DIE.

This is similar to the above, and will only do for a child under a week old.

Write the name of the father and mother, and the day the child was born upon a piece of blue paper, and put to every letter a number, beginning at 1, then add 15 to the total, and divide the whole by 5, if it is even, the child will die, on the other hand, if it is uneven, it will live.

CHARM OF THE RIBBONS.

OR HOW TO TELL WHETHER YOUR LOVER WILL MARRY YOU OR NOT.

Take two pieces of ribbon, precisely alike in length, breadth, and color, double each of them, separately, so that their ends meet, then join them together very neatly with a piece of silk of their own color by the middle or crease made in doubling them, by this you will have four ends to the ribbon, to this crease or join, fasten a wedding ring, previously borrowed from a woman, you must then borrow your lover's scarf-pin, which you must fasten in the wall, outside your bed-room window, then hang the ribbons on the pin, stretching one end upwards, one end downwards, and the other ends crosswise, to form a cross against the wall by the ends being fastened with pins. They must be where the sun shines, and should not be looked at for three hours, and if any of them fade or change color, your lover will be sure to marry you.

THE SULPHURIC CHARM.

OR HOW TO TELL A LADY IF SHE IS IN LOVE.

Put into a phial some sulphuric ether, color it red with orcharet, then mix the tincture with spermaceti, place the phial which contains it in a lady's hand, and if she is in love it will dissolve, and become fluid. This can be done at any time.

THE RING CHARM.

OR HOW TO FETCH YOUR LOVER TO YOU AT ANY REQUIRED TIME.

Prick your wedding finger of the left hand with a sharp needle till the blood flows, and with the blood write your own and lover's name on a piece of writing paper, encircle it with three round rings of the same crimson stream, fold it up, and exactly at the seventh hour of the evening, bury it in the earth, and tell no one, this done your lover will not be long before he makes an appearance.

CHARM WITH THE BREAD AND WINE.

OR HOW TO TELL WHETHER YOU WILL HAVE A FAMILY OR NOT.

Half fill a glass with water, throw a piece of bread into it, about the size of a nut; pour some wine lightly on the bread, and if you see the water at the bottom of the glass, and the wine floating at the top, you will have a family, but, if the wine mix with the water, you will not.

TO SEE A FUTURE HUSBAND OR SWEETHEART IN A DREAM.

The party inquiring must lie in a different county from that in which she resides, and on going to bed must knit the left garter about the right leg stocking, letting the other garter and stocking alone; as you rehearse the following verse knit a knot at every comma :—

> This knot I knit, to know the thing I know not yet,
> That I may see, the man that my husband shall be,
> How he goes, and what he wears,
> And what he does all days and years.

Accordingly, he will appear in a dream with the insignia of his trade or profession.

TO KNOW IF YOUR SWEETHEART WILL MARRY YOU.

Let any unmarried woman take the blade-bone of a shoulder of lamb, and borrowing a pen-knife, (but be sure not to mention for what purpose,) on going to bed stick the knife once through the bone for nine nights, in different places, repeating these words while sticking the knife :—

> 'Tis not this bone I mean to stick,
> But my lover's heart I mean to prick.
> Wishing him neither rest nor sleep,
> Till he comes to me to speak.

At the end of nine days or shortly after he will ask for something to put to a wound he will have met with during the time you were charming him.

TO KNOW WHETHER A FEMALE WILL HAVE THE MAN SHE WISHES.

Get two lemon peels, carry them about with you all day, one in each pocket; at night rub the four posts of the bedstead with them. If you are to succeed the person will appear in your sleep, and present you with a couple of lemons; if not there is no hope.

TO KNOW WHETHER A PERSON WILL BE MARRIED.

Take a pea-pod in which are nine peas, hang the same over the door, and take notice of the first person who comes in who is not of the family, and if he be a bachelor you will be married within the year.

THE HERB CHARM.

OR HOW TO MAKE A MAN LOVE YOU WHETHER HE IS PREVIOUSLY INCLINED TO DO SO OR NOT.

Place a sprig of red sage, a sprig of rosemary, or any other garden herb in a glass jar, so that when it is inverted, the stem may be downwards, and the sprig supported by the sides of the jar, then put some benzoic acid upon a piece of iron, so that the acid may be sublimed in the form of a thick white vapor. Invert the jar over the iron, and leave the whole untouched until the sprig be covered by the sublimed acid in the form of a beautiful hoar frost. This done you must bury the jar under an apple-tree, first covering the mouth of it with a piece of parchment, and on going to bed, and on getting up in the morning, you must repeat the following rhyme:

> O fragrant herbs I ask of thee,
> To make my chosen one love me,
> Let him not lead a happy life,
> Until I am his wedded wife.

Now, this charm or mystic spell is finished, beware of removing or looking at the jar until your chosen one has married you, or the charm will be broken.

THE FRIDAY AND MIDSUMMER CHARM.

On any Friday throughout the year take rosemary flowers, bay leaves, thyme, and sweet marjoram, of each a handful; dry these and make them into fine powder; then take a tea-spoonful of each sort, mix the whole together, then take twice the quantity of barley flour, and mix the whole into a cake with the milk of a red cow. This cake is not to be baked, but wrapped in clean writing-paper, and laid under your head at night. If the person dreams of music she will shortly wed him she wishes, if she dreams of fire she will be crossed in love, if of a church, she will die single. If anything is written or there is the least spot on the paper it will not do. Again:—

If any unmarried woman, fasting on Midsummer eve, and at midnight laying a clean cloth, with bread, cheese and ale, and sitting down as if going to eat (the street door being left open) the person whom she is afterwards to marry will come into the room and drink to her by bowing, and afterwards filling the glass, will leave it on the table, and making another bow retire.

TO FIND OUT THE TWO FIRST LETTERS OF A FUTURE WIFE OR HUSBAND'S NAME.

Take a small Bible and the key of the street-door, and having opened at Solomon's Songs, chap. viii. verses 6 and 7, place the wards of the key on those two verses and let the loop of the key be about an inch out of the top of the Bible, then shut the book and tie it round with your garter so as the key will not move, and the person who wishes to know his or her future husband or wife's signature must suspend the Bible by putting the middle finger of the right hand under the loop of the key, and the other person in the like manner on the other side of the key; then repeat the following passage, after the other person's saying the alphabet, one letter to each time repeating.

"Set me as a seal upon thine heart, as a seal upon thine arm, for love is strong as death, jealousy is cruel as the grave; the coals thereof are coals of fire, which hath a most vehement flame.

"Many waters cannot quench love, neither can the floods drown it; if a man would give all the substance of his house for love, it would utterly be contemned."

It must be observed that you mention to the person who repeats the verses, before you begin, which you intend to try first, whether the surname or christian name, and take care to hold the Bible steady. When you arrive at the appointed letter the book will turn round under your finger, and that you will find to be the first letter of your intended's name.

TO DISCOVER TRUTH FROM FALSEHOOD.

If you suspect your servant, or any other person of telling a lie, or false story, that may be to your prejudice, or otherwise, be not so rash as to charge them with it directly, but try the following rule of art, to inform you for a certainty of that which you can at present only surmise or suspect, without any real ground:—

Write the name of the party, and the name of the day the discourse took place, which you cannot believe, and then mind the following alphabet and figures :—

A	B	C	D	E	F	G	H
10	2	20	4	14	6	6	7

I	K	L	M	N	O	P	Q
20	11	11	12	4	14	6	16

R	S	T	V	X	Y	Z
18	18	10	2	2	4	14

Take the letters, and figures belonging to them that will make the name of the party suspected, as well as those that form the name of the day, to which add 26, then divide the whole by 7, should the remainder be odd, you may rest assured the party has told you an untruth, which you may charge them with, and either by open confession, blushes, or some other sign, you may easily discover the deception. But on the contrary, if it be even, you may rely on the truth of what has been told you.

MADAME JOHNSON'S METHOD FOR TELLING FOR TUNES BY LINES IN THE HAND.

Observe always to choose the left hand, because the heart and brain have more influence over it than the right hand; and observe further, it is better to examine these lines when the lady is in good health, for then they appear full.

By this the reader will see that one of the lines, and which indeed is reckoned the principal, is called the line of life; this line encloses the thumb, separating it from the hollow of the hand. The next to it, which is called the natural line, takes its beginning from the rising of the middle finger. The table line, commonly called the line of fortune, begins under the little finger, and ends near the forefinger. The girdle of Venus, another line so called, begins near the joint of the forefinger, and ends in the middle finger. The line of death is a counter line to the line of life, and is by some called the sister line. There are also lines in the fleshy parts, as in the ball of the thumb, which is called the mount of Venus, which are each governed by the several planets, and the hollow of the hand is called the place of Mars.

If the lines which are in the middle of the hand, and are called the table lines, are broad and fair, without being broken, it is a sure sign the parties will lead a happy life.

If the line from the wrist goes straight up to the little finger, it is a better sign than if broken, for then it denotes the party will live to a good old age; but on the contrary, should the line want continuity, they are in danger of sudden death.

If the line of life, which is that which runs from the wrist by the ball of the thumb, and ends directly under the forefinger, is clear, and ends without breaks, it denotes possession, prosperity, and happy old age. Round lines, like semicircles on the inside of the tips of the fingers, promise houses, land, and inheritance. As many lines or crosses as a woman has in her wrist, so many children she may expect to have.

If the middle or table lines, in the hand, are very narrow and contracted, it is a sign of poverty and crosses in the world. If a crooked line goes through the table line, it is a sign of death by accident or violence, but if it runs straight even through, it is a good sign.

THE ART OF TELLING FORTUNES BY THE GROUNDS OF TEA OR COFFEE.

Pour out the grounds of tea or coffee into a white cup; shake them well in it, and reverse it in the saucer. It is not to be expected that the figures will be accurately represented, but the more fertile the fancy shall be of the person inspecting the cup, the more he will discover in it.

The Roads, or serpentine lines, indicate ways; if they are covered with clouds and in the thick, they are marks of past or future reverses; but if in the clear and serene, are a token of some fortunate change; encompassed with many points or dots, they signify gain of money, likewise long life.

The Ring signifies marriage. If the ring is in the clear, it portends happiness; surrounded with clouds denotes that the party must use precaution lest they be deceived. It is most inauspicious if the ring appear at the bottom of the cup, as it forebodes separation.

The Anchor implies success in business if at bottom; at the top in the clear, love and constancy; in thick or cloudy parts, love, but inconstant.

The Coffin prognosticates long illness if it be in thick; in the clear, long life.

The Star, in the clear, denotes happiness; clouded or in the thick, it signifies long life; if dots are about it, it fortells fortune, wealth, honors, &c.

The Serpent is a sure sign of an enemy. On the top or in the middle shows victory over him, in the cloudy part it will not be so easy.

The Cross, be there one or more, predicts adversity. At the top, in the clear, denotes the party's misfortunes to be near an end.

The Heart. If in the clear, it signifies future pleasure; if surrounded with dots, it promises recovery of money; if two are together, it shows the party is about marrying.

The Rod shows difference with relations about legacies; in the thick, illness.

Flowers. If the party be married, he may expect good children, who will be a blessing to him in his old age.

Mountains. If only one, it indicates the favor of people of high rank; if clouded, powerful foes.

Fish imply lucky events by water, if in the clear; if in the thick, the consulter will fish in troubled water.

THE PERFECT FORTUNE TELLER.

MOLES.

A mole on the right side of the forehead, or right temple, signifies the person will arrive to sudden wealth and honor.

A mole on the right eyebrow foretells speedy marriage, the husband to possess good qualities and a large fortune.

A mole on the left of either of those three places portends unexpected disappointment in your most sanguine wishes.

A mole on the outside of either eye, denotes the person to be of a steady, sober, sedate disposition.

A mole on either cheek, signifies that the person never shall rise above mediocrity in point of fortune.

A mole on the nose shows the that person will have good success in his or her undertakings.

A mole on the chin indicates prosperity.

A mole on the side of the neck shows the person will narrowly escape suffocation; but will afterwards rise to honor.

A mole on the throat, denotes that the person shall become rich by marriage.

A mole on the right breast indicates the person to be exposed to a sudden reverse from comfort to distress.

A mole on the left breast, signifies success in undertakings.

A mole on the bosom signifies health and fortune.

A mole under the left breast, over the heart, shows that a man will be of a warm disposition and unsettled in mind. In a lady, it shows sincerity in love, and easy travail in childbirth.

A mole on the right side over any part of the ribs, denotes the person to be pusillanimous, and slow in understanding.

A mole on the belly shows the person to be addicted to sloth and gluttony, and not very choice in point of dress.

A mole on the hip shows the person will have many children.

A mole on the right thigh is an indication of riches.

A mole on the left thigh denotes poverty and want of friends.

A mole on the right knee shows the person will be fortunate in the choice of a partner for life.

A mole on the left knee portends that the person will be rash, inconsiderate and hasty, but modest when in cool blood.

A mole on either ankle denotes a man to be inclined to effeminacy—a lady, to be active, with trifle of termagant.

A mole on either foot forebodes unexpected misfortune.

A mole on the right shoulder indicates prudence and wisdom.

A mole on the left shoulder declares a testy, contentious, and ungovernable spirit.

A mole on the right arm denotes vigor and courage.

A mole on the left arm shows resolution and victory in battle.

A mole near either elbow, denotes restlessness, with those which they are obliged to live constantly with.

A mole between the elbow and the wrist promises the person prosperity, but not until he has undergone many hardships.

A mole on the wrist, or between it and the end of the fingers, shows industry, parsimony, and conjugal affection.

A mole on any part from the shoulders to the loins, is indicative of unperceptible decline and gradual decay, whether of health or wealth.

CONCERNING CHILDREN BORN ON ANY DAY OF THE WEEK.

Sunday.—The child born on Sunday will obtain great riches, and be long-lived and happy.

THE PERFECT FORTUNE TELLER.

Monday.—Not very successful, irreso͏͏͏͏͏ subject to be imposed on, good-natured, and willing to do every ·hing in his power.

Tuesday.—The person born will be subject to violent starts of passion, and not easily reconciled.

Wednesday.—Will be given to study, and excel in literature.

Thursday.—The child born will attain great riches and honor, and will be of a sanguine temperament.

Friday.—The child born will be of a strong constitution.

Saturday.—Is an unlucky day, but the child may come to good, though generally of an evil disposition.

INFORMATION FOR MOTHERS, ON THE POWER OF THE RULING PLANETS, AND THE FATE OF THEIR OFFSPRING.

ARIES, from 21st March to 19th April, inclusive.
 Aries, or the Ram; ruler of congenial spring,
 Now invites you to rejoice, and o'er your child sing,
 Successful business and money it doth presage,
 Also a courageous temper, health and old age.

TAURUS, from 20th April to 20th May, inclusive.
 If under Taurus, the Bull, male children are born,
 Fond of farms and vineyards, they'll gather fruit and corn,
 Will delight in singing and pleasure, and fine dress,
 Females born under this sign, meet little success.

GEMINI, from 21st May to 21st June, inclusive.
 Gemini, or Twins, bestow in children good parts,
 They will incline to wisdom and the fine arts,
 Great abilities they will show, and learn with ease,
 Be fond of good company, and with their wit please.

CANCER, from 22d June to 22d July, inclusive.
 Cancer, the Crab, is an acute and subtle sign,
 A babe with an inventive genius shall be thine,

Three-one. A great discovery is at hand

Three-blank. An illegitimate child.

Double-two. You will have a jealous partner.

Two-one. You will soon find something to your advantage in the street or road.

Two-blank. You will lose money or some article of value.

Double-one. The loss of a friend, whom you will very much miss.

One-blank. You are being closely watched by one whom you little expect.

Double-blank. The worst presage in all the set; you will meet trouble from a quarter for which you are quite unprepared.

It is useless for persons to draw more than three dominoes at one time of trial, or in one and the same week, as they will only deceive themselves. Shuffle the dominoes each time of choosing.

AUGURY BY DICE.

Take three dice, shake them well in the box with your left hand, and then cast them out on a board or table, on which you have previously drawn a circle with chalk.

Three. A pleasing surprise.

Four. A disagreeable one.

Five. A stranger who will prove a **friend.**

Six. Loss of property.

Seven. Undeserved scandal.

Eight. merited reproach.

Nine. A wedding.

Ten. A christening.

Eleven. A death that concerns you.

Twelve. A letter speedily.

Thirteen. Tears and Sighs.

Fourteen. Beware that you are not drawn into some trouble or plot by a secret enemy.

Fifteen. Immediate prosperity and happiness.

Sixteen. A pleasant journey.

Seventeen. You will either be on the water, or have dealings with those belonging to it, to your advantage.

Eighteen. A great profit, rise in life, or some most desirable good will happen almost immediately.

To show the same number twice at one trial, portends news from abroad, be the number what it may. If the dice roll over the circle, the number thrown goes for nothing, but the occurrence shows sharp words; and if they fall to the floor, it is blows. In throwing out the dice, if one remains on the top of the other, it is an omen of which I would have them take care.

THE EGYPTIAN CIRCLE;

OR,

Ancient Wheel of Fortune.

THE EGYPTIAN CIRCLE;

OR,

ANCIENT WHEEL OF FORTUNE.

The Egyptian Circle was much used by the ancients, who were pious and devout men. They always duly observed the same rules and directions in respect to their qualification and preparation in noble science, as they did in the science of Geomancy.

THE EGYPTIAN CIRCLE SHOWS:

1. Whether you shall obtain the favor of the person you desire?

2. If the querent shall meet with the preferment he wisheth for?

3. Whether a sick person will recover?

4. If the said sickness will be long or short?

5. Shall your expectation or wish succeed?

6. If it is good for you to marry, or otherwise?

7. Whether the friendship of a certain person will prove advantageous or not?

8. Whether a person shall be rich or poor? &c., &c.

RULE.—The person whose fortune is to be told, must place the Wheel of Fortune face downwards, prick it into a number (with the eyes shut), then refer for an explanation, which stands at the corresponding number as that you pricked into.

The following observations answer for either sex the party, herefore, trying this Wheel, must alter wife for husband, or ust as the answers may suit either party:

THE PERFECT FORTUNE TELLER.

1. If this number is fixed upon, it assures the person that you will marry a homely person, but rich.

2. Whatever your intentions are, for the present decline them. Those absent will return.

3. Shows loss of friends ; bad success at law ; loss of money, unfaithfulness in love.

4. If your desires are extravagant, they will not be granted ; but mind how you make use of your fortune.

5. Very good fortune ; sudden prosperity ; great respect from high personages ; a letter bringing important news.

6. Look well to those who owe you money, if ever so little; a letter of abuse may be expected.

7. Your lover will act constant and true towards you.

8. A friend has crossed the sea and will bring home riches, by which you will be much benefited.

9. A loving partner ; success in your undertakings ; a large and prosperous family.

10. Your husband will not have a great fortune, but with assistance is likely to live in middling circumstances.

11. A very sudden journey with a pleasant fellow-traveler, and the result of the journey will be generally beneficial to your family.

12. You may regain that which you have lost with great perseverance and trouble.

13. A letter of importance will arrive, announcing the death of a relative for whom you have no very great respect, but who has left you a legacy.

14. By venturing carefully you will gain doubly, though you will suffer great privation.

15. You will meet with many crosses before you are comfortably settled.

16. Too sudden acqaintance with the opposite sex but which will be opposed ; notwithstanding the party should persevere, as it will be to his or her advantage.

THE PERFECT FORTUNE TELLER.

17. An agreeable partner, a good temper, and a large family of children.

18. Let the chooser of this number persevere; for your schemes are good, and must succeed.

19. You will marry young, and have dutiful children.

20. Your lover may be low in circumstances, but affectionate.

21. Your marriage will add to your welfare, and you will be very happy.

22. A drunken partner, bad success in trade, but the party will never be very poor, though always unhappy.

23. Do not neglect your lover; let your conduct command respect.

24. You have many friends, and will probably have a large and virtuous family.

25. Your travels will be prosperous, if you are prudent.

26. You have many enemies who will endeavor to make you unhappy.

27. The luck that is ordained for you will be coveted by others.

28. Be very prudent in your conduct, as this number is very precarious, and much depends upon yourself; it is generally good.

29. Beware, or you will be deceived by the person you are paying your attentions to.

30. You love one who is affectionate and true, and deserves respect.

31. You too fantastically refuse offers. Be prudent when you accept, or you will be sorry.

32. You will be very unfortunate for a short time, but be careful, and your situation will very soon alter.

33. A fortune will be yours, but be not over anxious.

34. Alter your intentions, or you will be sorry when it is too late.

35. You will have a rich but jealous partner, and will live very uncomfortable.

36. You will have a sober, steady, and affectionate partner, but poor.

37. A very good fortune, sudden prosperity, and a large family.

38. The person who choses this unlucky number mnst look well to their conduct, or justice will overtake them.

39. Remain among your friends, then you will escape misfortune.

40. You will have an affectionate partner, but no family; and a large fortune.

41. If you have a fortune, be charitable; if but little, be frugal.

42. You will have a quarrel with your lover through jealousy.

43. You must bear your losses with fortitude.

44. You will get a handsome, young, wealthy partner.

45. When your conduct changes, your fortune will mend, by marrying a rich partner.

46. You have mixed with bad company, and you may depend on it that you will be brought to disgrace.

47. A large family of healthy children, give them learning, and they will honor their father and mother.

48. You will be very unfortunate at first, but persevere and your schemes will be successful.

49. You have a number of secret enemies who will try to do you an injury; be on your guard and you will prosper.

50. Your happiness will consist in doing good ; they are pleasing spots in the memory which vexations cannot erase.

51. You will die an old maid; you have been too whimsical in choosing for yourself a partner.

52. Your lover will travel on the continent, and will be very successful.

53. You will marry a person with whom you will have but little comfort.

54. This is a very lucky number, whatever you do will always prove successful.

55. After much misfortune, you will be pretty comfortable and happy.

56. Good conduct will produce much luck and happiness.

57. Through affection you will marry unfortunately, but you must make one another happy.

58. You have many lovers, but mind how you choose, or else you will suffer for it.

59. Your lover is on his return home.

60. A letter announcing loss of money.

61. You have a secret enemy, mind or he will do you some harm.

62. Warns you against the evil consequences of idleness either in yourself or partner.

63. Your partner will be very rich, but very neglectful.

64. You will be very poor and miserable with one child.

65. Sincere love from an upright heart will be rewarded.

66. You will marry an old person with whom you will be very happy.

67. Plenty of offers will happen before one is worthy of acceptance, be cautious how you make your choice.

68. You will play with the mouse till till you lose it.

69. Take heed, you are being deceived by your lover.

70. You will meet with great trouble, you should have consulted your friends.

71. Beware, the person you love does not love you, he seeks your ruin.

72. If you marry in haste you will be deceived; wait patiently and you will be happy.

73. Hard work, hard fare, little joy, and much care.

74. A scolding wife, but rich.

75. Your parner will be very rich, but will have no children.

76. You have a rival, be not deceived; depend on our tablets, and you will better your condition.

77. You will have many children, but will be very poor.

78. Do not delay, hasten your marriage, or you will lose your virtue.

79. Your wife will have no children, and will be addicted to drinking liquors.

80. Be honest and industrious and you will triumph over your enemies.

81. You will have children, who, if you give them good education, will make you happy.

82. You will fall into great difficulties, you will lose your partner and marry a drunkard.

83. Hasten your marriage, the person is faithful, and you will be happy.

84. You must break off the connection you have formed, or you will come to absolute want.

85. Your lover is jealous of you, and will break of the connection.

86. You will travel on the continent and be married there, but will have no children.

87. You will get married, but not till you begin to get old.

88. Beware, you have a secret enemy, who will try and do you some injury.

89. You will die an old maid.

90. You will marry three different times, and still be very poor and miserable.

91. The person you are paying your attentions to is deceitful.

92. If you marry you will have great trouble and many children; be persuaded, and live single, then you will be happy.

93. You will live to a great age and be happy.

94. There is a young man dying in love for you, but mind you are not led astray.

95. You will marry poor, but in the end be rich.

96. You are too whimsical and deceitful ever to be happy.

97. Be not flattered, for you have an amorous sweetheart.

98. A shocking accident will happen to you, or to your children, which will cause great trouble.

99. You will discover your false lover.

100. You will have a very handsome, but artful partner.

GREEK FIRE AND OTHER ANCIENT MYSTERIES.

The Rabbins, given up to the study of the Cabbala, speak of a light belonging to saints, to the elect, upon whose countenance it shines miraculously from their birth, or when they have merited this sign of glory. Arnobus, on the authority of Hermippus, gives to the magician Zoroaster a belt of fire; a suitable ornament for the institutor of the worship of fire. A philosopher of the present age would be very little embarrassed how to produce these brilliant wonders, particularly if their duration was not required to be much prolonged.

The Druids extended the resources of science much farther. The renowned person, who, in the poem of Lucan, proclaims their magical power, boasts of possessing the secret of making a forest appear on fire, when it does not burn. Ossian paints old men, mixed with the sons of Loda, and at night making conjurations round a cromlech, or circle of stones; and, at their command, burning meteors arose, which terrified the warriors of Fingal, and by the light of which Ossian distinguished the chief of the enemy's warriors. An English translation of Ossian observes that every bright flame, sudden, and resembling lightning, is called in Gaelic, the Druid's flame. It is to this flame that Ossian compares the sword of his son Oscar. Connected with the recital of the bard, this expression indicates that the Druids possessed the art of causing flames to appear, for the purpose of dismaying their enemies.

We may join to the traits of resemblance already observed between the Celts and the ancient inhabitants of Italy, the fable of Cæculus, the founder of the city of Preneste. Wishing to make himself known as the son of the god Vulcan, he implored the aid of his sire, when suddenly an assembled multitude, who had refused to acknowledge his brilliant origin, were enveloped in flames, and the alarm quickly subdued their incredulity.

We may remark, that Cæculus, most probably, had chosen the place of assembly, and that the Druids only exercised their power in sacred enclosures, interdicted to the profane, as in certain optical illusions where fire has often played a part; for these apparent miracles required a theater suitab'e to those who worked them; and, in other places, in spite of the urgency of necessity, they would have experienced great difficulty in any attempt to produce them.

The instantaneous development of latent heat is not less likely to excite astonishment, particularly if water kindles the flames. Substances susceptible of evolving heat, or of taking fire, in absorbing or in decomposing water, are numerous, and they have very often occasioned fires, such as were attributed, formerly, to negligence or to malice. Stacks of damp hay, and slates of pyrites, moistened by a warm shower, will produce this phenomenon.

Were the Thaumaturgists acquainted with phenomena similar to the latter? I reply, without doubt, they were. The prodigious heat which is emitted by quicklime sprinkled with water could not have escaped their observation. Now, let us suppose that a sufficient quantity of quicklime is hidden at the bottom of a pit, or kiln, and that the pit is then filled with snow; the absorbed snow will disappear, and the interior temperature of the pit or kiln will be so much more raised, owing to its being thus closely shut, that less of the expanded heat will be allowed to escape—and an apparent miracle will be proclaimed. Thus, a writer of legends has ornamented the history of St. Patrick, by relating that the apostle of Ireland lighted a kiln with snow.

Theophrastus gives the name of spinon to a stone which is met with in certain mines, and which, if pounded, and then exposed to the sun, ignites of itself, particularly if care has been taken to wet it first. The spinon, there can be little doubt, is merely an efflorescing pyrites. The stone named gagates (true pyritic jet) is black, porous, light, friable, and resembles burned wood. It exhales a disagreeable odor, and, when it is heated, it attracts other bodies in the same manner as amber. The smoke which it exhales in burning relieves women attacked with hysterics, and it is kindled by means of water, and extinguished when immersed in oil. The latter peculiarity was also the distinguishing feature of a stone which, according to Ælian and Dioscorides, ignited in a like manner, when sprinkled with water, and, in burning, exhaled a strong bituminous smell; but, as it was extinguished by blowing above it, its combustion seems to have depended on the escape of a gaseous vapor.

Those three substances, whether they were the productions

of art or of nature, might have sufficed to work miraculous conflagrations. But Pliny and Isidore of Seville have described a fourth, still more powerful—a black stone that is found in Persia, and which, if broken between the fingers, burns them. This is precisely the effect produced by a bit of pyrophorus, or phosphorus stone, and this wonderful stone was probably nothing else. It is known that phosphorus, melted by heat, may become black and solid, and the word stone ought not to impose more upon us here than the words lake and fountain when a liquid is spoken of. Custom has consecrated in our own language the words infernal stone (*lapis infernalis*) and cauterizing stone, for a pharmaceutical preparation.

But were the ancients acquainted with phosphorus and pyrophorus? I reply in the affirmative, since they relate wonders which could have been produced by no other means than the employment of these substances, or by reactives, endowed with analogous properties. We shall have occasion to mention an ancient description of the effects of a combination of phosphorus, a description as exact as if it had been made at the present time by a modern chemist. As to pyrophorus, science possesses so many substances which ignite after some minutes' exposure to the air, that it may, without improbability, be believed that many of them were known to the ancients. Without mentioning bitumens as being highly inflammable, or petroleum, or naphtha, which take fire at the approach of a lighted candle, how many of the residue of distillations kindle spontaneously in a damp atmosphere. This property, to which no attention is paid, except to explain it by a general principle, was certainly never neglected by the performers of apparent miracles, since the art of distillation formed an important part of the sacred sciences.

We will not then hesitate to believe, though it may well astonish us, what history relates of a vestal threatened with the punishment reserved for those who allowed the sacred fire to go out, that she had only to spread her veil over the altar in order that the flame should suddenly rekindle, and burn more vividly than before. From beneath the friendly veil, we may imagine that we perceive a grain of phosphorus or of pyrophorus to fall on the hot cinders, and supply the place of the intervention of the divinity.

Nor need we longer share the incredibility of Horace, respecting the apparent miracle which was worked in the sanctuary of Gnatia, where the incense kindled of itself in honor of the gods. We also may understand how Seleucus, sacrificing to Jupiter, saw the wood-pile upon the altar ignite spontaneously to offer a brilliant presage of his future greatness; neither can we deny that the Theurgist Maximus, offering incense to Hecate, might have been able to announce that the torches which the goddess held would light themselves spontaneously, and that his prediction had been accomplished.

Notwithstanding the precautions which the love of mystery inspired, and which was seconded by the enthusiasm of admiration, the working of the science was sometimes openly shown in its assumed miracles. Pausanias relates what he saw in two cities of Lydia, the inhabitants of which, subjected to the yoke of the Persians, had embraced the religion of the Magi. "In a chapel," he says, "is an altar, upon which there are always *ashes, that in color do not resemble* any others. That Magi placed some wood upon the altar, and invoked I know not what god, by orisons taken from a book written in a barbarous language unknown to the Greeks; the wood soon ignited of itself without fire, and the flame of it was very brilliant."

The extraordinary color of the cinders, which were always kept upon the altar; doubtlessly concealed an inflammable composition; simply, perhaps, earth soaked in petroleum or naphtha—a species of fuel still employed in Persia, in every place where these bituminous substances are common. The Magi, in placing the wood, probably threw there, without its being perceived, a few grains of pyrophorus, or of that stone which was found in Persia, and which was kindled by a light pressure. While the orison lasted, the action of either substance had time to develop itself.

The vine-branches which a priest placed upon an altar, near Agrigentum, lighted spontaneously in the same manner. Solinus adds, that the flame ascended from the altar toward the assistants without incommoding them. The circumstance announces that between the vine-branches a gas escaped, and was lighted from below the altar, in a manner similar to that at Mount Eryx, where a perpetual flame is preserved on the altar of Venus. The fumes of a spirituous liquor would have produced the same phenomenon. By the inflammation of an ethereal fluid, also, may be explained the power that Fromann attributes to the Zingari of making fire appear upon a single bundle of straw placed among many others, and of extinguishing it at pleasure. In this manner school-boys amuse themselves by making alcohol burn in their hands; a puff of breath disperses the flame at the moment when they begin to feel the heat of it.

"It has been observed," says Buffon, "that some substances thrown up by Ætna, after having been cooled during several years and then moistened with rain, have rekindled and thrown off flames, with an explosion violent enough to pro duce even a slight earthquake." The composition of these volcanic productions may have been imitated by art, or the Thaumaturgist may have carefully collected and preserved those which nature had formed. One of the four stones inflammable by water, of which we have spoken, shall be explained elsewhere.

In fact we may remark, with a man whom science and his country have equally regretted, that quicklime mixed with sulphur, by the heat which it emits when sprinkled with water, first fuses, and then causes the combustion of the sulphur; that this mixture rapidly sets on fire mixed with sulphur and chlorate of potassa, and suddenly ignites gunpowder and phosphorus; and that, in the latter case, there exists a physical means of fixing the precise moment when the developed heat will cause the combustion.

Let us transport ourselves among a people whose first historical centuries, owing to the marvelous recitals with which they are filled, are thrown back into the indefinite ages of mythology.

The impartial reader will follow us in the march of these recitals. Let him weigh well all the expressions which Dejanira employs for describing the first effects of the *Blood of Nessus*, a marvellous philter, with which she impregnated the precious tunic that was to bring back the heart of her inconstant husband. "Nessus," says she, advised me to keep this liquid in a dark place until the moment when I wished to make use of it. This is what I have done. To-day, *in the dark*, with a flock of wool dipped in the liquid, I have dyed the tunic which I have sent, after having shut it in a box, without *its having been exposed to the light*. The flock of wool, exposed to the sun upon a stone, was spontaneously consumed, without having been touched by any one. It was reduced to ashes, into a powder resembling that which the saw causes to fall from wood. I have observed that above the stone on which I had placed it froth bubbles appeared, like those which, in autumn, are produced from wine poured from a height."

Let a chemist read these details, stripped of all mythological recollections; what will he recognize in this pretended philter, given by the hand of vengeance, and which, from its consistence, color, or some other property, received the appellation of blood? I reply, a liquid preparation of phosphorus, which, owing to the proportions of its elements, inflamed spontaneously when it was exposed to the light and heat of the sun. The phosphoric acid produced from its combustion would produce upon the stone the effervescence which struck the eyes of

Dejanira, and also the ashes of the wool reduced to dry and insoluble phosphate.

Hercules clothed himself with the fatal tunic; then he sacrificed twelve bulls; but scarcely had he taken the fire to the wood-pile on which the victims were deposited, than he felt the effects of the philter. The vicinity of the flame, the chemist will say, and the humid heat of the skin of a man who works with strength and activity before a kindled pile will infallibly determine, though without visible inflammation, the decomposition of the phosphoret spread upon the garment. The compound being dried up, and therefore much more caustic, would act upon all parts of the body, disorganize the skin and the flesh, and, by inexpressible pains, cause the death of its unfortunate victim. Even at this day, when its nature is not unknown, it would be difficult to arrest the action once begun of these consuming substances; **formerly it would have been impossible.**

Arabi Manor

www.arabimanor.com

DOUBLE FAST LUCK

ALLEDGED
GOOD LUCK

HIGH QUALITY

OILS

INCENSE

CANDLES

Arabi Manor Esoterica is Rebel Satori's full line of handcrafted and carefully curated magickal supplies, books and esoteric ephemera.

SOAPS

BOOKS

TAROT CARDS

AND MORE

SPECIAL NO. 20

www.ingramcontent.com/pod-product-compliance
Lightning Source LLC
Chambersburg PA
CBHW031134090426
42738CB00008B/1086